Farewell to Work?

Studies in
Critical Social Sciences

Series Editor
David Fasenfest (*Wayne State University*)

Editorial Board
Eduardo Bonilla-Silva (*Duke University*)
Chris Chase- Dunn (*University of California-Riverside*)
William Carroll (*University of Victoria*)
Raewyn Connell (*University of Sydney*)
Kimberlé W. Crenshaw (*University of California, LA,* and
Columbia University)
Raju Das (*York University*)
Heidi Gottfried (*Wayne State University*)
Karin Gottschall (*University of Bremen*)
Alfredo Saad-Filho (*King's College London*)
Chizuko Ueno (*University of Tokyo*)
Sylvia Walby (*Lancaster University*)

VOLUME 198

The titles published in this series are listed at *brill.com/scss*

Farewell to Work?

Essays on the World of Work's Metamorphoses and Centrality

By

Ricardo Antunes

Translated by

Murillo van der Laan and others

BRILL

LEIDEN | BOSTON

Cover illustration: Adeus ao Trabalho? (Farewell to Work?) by Ricardo Rezende, especially for the English edition of *Adeus ao Trabalho*.

Library of Congress Cataloging-in-Publication Data

Names: Antunes, Ricardo, 1953- author.
Title: Farewell to work? : essays on the world of work's metamorphoses and centrality / by Ricardo Antunes ; translated by Murillo van der Laan and others.
Other titles: Adeus ao trabalho? English
Description: Leiden ; Boston : Brill, [2022] | Series: Studies in critical social sciences, 1573-4234 ; vol. 198 | Includes bibliographical references and index. | Summary: "Farewell to Work? presents the large process of capital's productive restructuring, triggered in the 1970s. A process with tendencies to both intellectualize labour power and increase the levels of working class' precariousness, on a global scale. Its main hypothesis is that instead of work's loss of centrality in contemporary capitalism, when the world of production is analysed in its global dimension, including countries in North and South, a substantial process of growing heterogeneity, complexity and fragmentation is observed. This configures a new morphology of the working class. Therefore, at the same time that new mechanisms are created to generate surplus labour, there is, simultaneously, an increment in casualisation and unemployment, pushed by a process of corrosion of labour rights"– Provided by publisher.
Identifiers: LCCN 2021045761 (print) | LCCN 2021045762 (ebook) |
    ISBN 9789004465589 (hardback ; alk. paper) | ISBN 9789004466067 (ebook)
Subjects: LCSH: Labor. | Working class. | Labor movement.
Classification: LCC HD4904 .A57613 2021 (print) | LCC HD4904 (ebook) |
    DDC 331.01–dc23
LC record available at https://lccn.loc.gov/2021045761
LC ebook record available at https://lccn.loc.gov/2021045762

Typeface for the Latin, Greek, and Cyrillic scripts: "Brill". See and download: brill.com/brill-typeface.

ISSN 1573-4234
ISBN 978-90-04-46558-9 (hardback)
ISBN 978-90-04-46606-7 (e-book)

Copyright 2022 by Koninklijke Brill NV, Leiden, The Netherlands.
Koninklijke Brill NV incorporates the imprints Brill, Brill Nijhoff, Brill Hotei, Brill Schöningh, Brill Fink, Brill mentis, Vandenhoeck & Ruprecht, Böhlau Verlag and V&R Unipress.
All rights reserved. No part of this publication may be reproduced, translated, stored in a retrieval system, or transmitted in any form or by any means, electronic, mechanical, photocopying, recording or otherwise, without prior written permission from the publisher. Requests for re-use and/or translations must be addressed to Koninklijke Brill NV via brill.com or copyright.com.

This book is printed on acid-free paper and produced in a sustainable manner.

So they carry on with their daily lives, each in his own way, reflecting and not reflecting. Everything seems to be going on as it always does. Because even in momentous times, when everything is at stake, you do go on with your daily life as if nothing is happening.
GOETHE (*Elective Affinities*)

Contents

Foreword IX
Preface to the English Edition XII
About *Farewell to Work?* XV
Acknowledgements XVII
List of Tables XVIII

Introduction 1

PART 1
Heterogeneity and Fragmentation of the Working Class

1 Fordism, Toyotism and Flexible Accumulation 5

2 Metamorphoses in the World of Work 24

3 Dimensions of the Trade Unionism's Contemporary Crisis
Dilemmas and Challenges 37

4 Which Crisis of Labour Society? 47
   1 First Thesis 47
   2 Second Thesis 54
   3 Third Thesis 58
   4 Fourth Thesis 60
   5 Fifth Thesis 62

PART 2
Labour's New Morphology

5 The Explosion of the New Services Proletariat of the Digital Age 67
   1 The End of the Myth 67
   2 Service Work and Marx's Fundamental Clues 70
   3 Can Immaterial Labour Generate Surplus Value? 74
   4 Middle Class, Precariat or the New Service Proletariat? 77

6 Freeze-Dried Flexibility
   A New Morphology of Labour: Casualisation and Value   83
   1   Introduction   83
   2   Brazil in the New International Division of Labour   88
   3   The New Forms of Labour and Value: Tangibility and Intangibility   90
   4   The Design of the New Morphology of Labour   93

7 The Working Class Today
   The New Form of Being of the Class-that-lives-from-Labour   96

8 The Crisis Seen Globally
   Robert Kurz and the Collapse of Modernization   105
   1   An Explosive Book   105
   2   And Its Main Gaps   110

9 The International Working Class in 1864 and Today   116
   1   Introduction   116
   2   The New Morphology of Labour: Informality, Casualisation, Infoproletariat, and Value   118
   3   Conclusion   126

   Master References   129
   Index   134

Foreword

by Alain Bihr

In the age where the internet and the so-called 'new economy' are everywhere, labour is not on headlines anymore.[1] At best, we still know and recognize it from the standpoint of its computerisation. The moment would definitely be that of communication and informational interaction and no longer of the Promethean effort to make oneself 'master and possessor of nature', according to the Cartesian formula. This is the latest version of a postmodern theme that, for almost twenty years, has taken place at the end of the century and millennium under the banner of the 'end of work' and the 'farewell to workers.'

With this work, Ricardo Antunes deliberately places himself in conflict with the dominant ideology. Without falling into the latter's facilities, its schematic form little-inclined to argument, which simply reiterates that its strength comes from repetition and media amplification, here the author presents a detailed analysis of the changes currently affecting labour's reality, both objectively and subjectively.

From these transformations, Antunes strives, above all, to grasp the dialectical complexity, the unity of opposites and even contradictory movements that characterize them. There has been a de-proletarianization of industrial labour in core capitalist countries, followed by a relative and absolute reduction in the size of the traditional working class. Simultaneously, there has also been an increase in sub-proletarianization of part of industrial work and, particularly, of the tertiary sector, due to the development of subcontracting and precarious labour, not to mention the 'informal economy' or the 'underground economy', not restricted to peripheral countries. To further complicate matters, aligned with the computerisation of labour processes that rule the new paradigm of the fluid and flexible factory – which tends to replace the old Fordist factory – we witness the re-skilling and, consequently, the complexification of a part of the industrial work that was reduced to simple labour (in the sense that Marx employs these different terms).

Accordingly, the predominant idea Antunes advances is not that of an 'end of work', but of the fragmentation and heterogeneity within the world of work, and consequently of workers themselves. Essentially, in regards to the ideology of the 'end of work' Ricardo Antunes presents what it is, without a doubt, a

---

1 Translated by Henrique Amorim and edited by Murillo van der Laan.

definitive refutation, demonstrating that it rests on the misunderstanding of concrete and abstract labour (which brings us back, once again, to Marx). If one can speak of the 'end of work', it is not in the sense of the end of concrete labour, the end of social appropriation of nature, which, as a fundamental anthropological dimension, as an institution of social norm and language is intended to be what it has always been: the base on which social life is built. One can consider that, as labour productivity grows at the pace of accumulation of social means of production, the part of the 'concrete labour' in the lives of human beings decreases.

However, this is also what allows one to distinguish, within the ongoing changes, the premises of the end of 'abstract labour' – labour reduced to the substance of value, submitted therefore to market and monetary abstraction – thus, realizing the famous Marxian prophecy in the *Grundrisse*. If Ricardo Antunes deserves any criticism, it is because he showed a way, but did not systematically pursued and explored it. If so, he would have clarified the limits and contradictions of the current process of capitalist industrial automation.

As for those who waved farewell to workers and to the 'class-that-lives-from-labour' (as he renames the proletariat), Ricardo Antunes shows how they did it too soon. Undoubtedly, the changes currently affecting labour processes and production relations have an impact on workers. Antunes shows that such transformations have changed the material conditions of the proletariat's labour and life, their professional or political composition and their class consciousness. Against those who believe in being able to extract, from the numerical contradiction of the old European or American working classes, arguments for predicting the disappearance of the proletariat, Ricardo Antunes – keen observer of Brazilian industrialization and trade union movements – reiterates that the future of the proletariat must, from now on, be considered based on the extension of capitalist production relations that are simultaneously a product, agent and cause of the dissolution worldwide. At this scale, the proletariat is increasing rapidly and constantly.

However, it is also at this scale that, more than ever, the current fragmentation and heterogeneity of the proletariat imposes itself. Therefore, the inevitable question of how to bring unity among the scattered fragments of a worldwide working class, separated by geography and also by history, given the heterogeneity of ethnic, civilizational, religious, national and political traditions must be addressed. Facing the globalization of capital, how can labour be globalized, not only as an objective reality, dominated and exploited by capital, but as an antagonistic pole, a subjective reality, a class not only in-itself, but also for-itself?

FOREWORD   XI

In short, this is the question, not intended to be answered, which Ricardo Antunes finally reaches. The usefulness of his work focuses on the direction and putting forth means to a possible solution for the readers.

Preface to the English Edition

It is with great pleasure that we present the English edition of our book *Adeus ao Trabalho?* originally published in Brazil. Not only have several editions been printed in Portuguese (almost 20), but they have also been printed in other languages, now there are three editions in Italy, two in Argentina, two in Venezuela, one in Galicia, one in Colombia and one in Mexico. The publication of *Adeus ao Trabalho?* in English, many years after the original edition, is due to the fact that its fundamental thesis still seems to be valid nowadays, when we consider the world of work in its totality.

From the start, the central formulation in the book is a clear refusal of the theses that defended work's loss of centrality and relevance in contemporary capitalism. Our findings at the time essentially pointed out that there was a large process of *structural casualisation of labour on the global scale*. Human labour cannot be completely eliminated in the law of value and the system of capital, but its incorporation depends less and less on stable and formalized labour. Consequently, the number of precarious, flexible and deregulated work increased. What seemed to be the exception (informal and precarious labour) tended to become the rule, while regulated labour, endowed with rights, tended to decrease. This was our first analytical finding in *Adeus ao Trabalho?*

In our clear opposition to the theses about the 'end of work', we indicate the imperious need to better comprehend labour's new modes, its *new morphology*, which presents itself as an increasing participant in *social labour* and in the new chains of value production.

Instead of Eurocentrically claiming the 'end of work', it was necessary to study labour globally, given the huge differences between the North and South. Apprehending in this way its main tendencies, it was possible to understand the ongoing expressive metamorphoses within the world of work, which were becoming more *complex, heterogeneous, fragmented* and also more *intense* in its rhythms and processes.

The book also tried to emphasize the need to better understand the transformations coming from the expansion of the digital-informational universe, responsible for new forms of interaction between *living* and *dead labour*. This led us to note that we were experiencing both an increasing complexification and amplification (and not a reduction or elimination) of the law of value, in the opposite direction of a wide set of formulations, most of them coming from core capitalist countries, that defended the loss of relevance of the labour theory of value – in the new stage of the 'knowledge society', the 'service society' – that would tend to make labour irrelevant.

Predominantly Eurocentric, these theses were incapable of comprehending the transformations within the class-that-lives-from-labour (a conception I first developed in *Adeus ao Trabalho?*). Furthermore, an effective perception of the different processes and movements inside the working-class led us to study countries such as Brazil, Mexico, South Africa, China and India, among the many others in the periphery of capitalism.

The book also presented the perspective of the integration and insertion (and not independence) of immaterial labour in the logic of capital's valorisation, which also helped to indicate the theoretical fragility of the thesis that said *science became the main productive force, replacing living labour*. We put forward an alternative hypothesis which claimed it would be necessary to comprehend the new relational forms of interaction between *living* and *dead labour*.

Finally, *Adeus ao Trabalho?* also advanced an alternative reading of trade unions crisis (first in Global North and then in the South) and the necessity to rethink its forms of collective action, since a *new morphology of work* would tend to demand also a *new morphology* of forms of organization, representation and resistance from the working-class. These are the theses that constitute the core of *Adeus ao Trabalho?*, which were later analysed in the books *The Meanings of Work* (Brill Books, 2013 e Haymarket Books, 2013) and *O Privilégio da Servidão* (Boitempo, 2018, Punto Rosso, 2020).

The chapters that form the *first part* of *Adeus ao Trabalho?* (chapters 1 to 4) kept their original form, first published in Brazil in 1995 and, more recently, in Italy under the title *Addio al Lavoro? Le matamorfosi e la centralità del Lavoro*, in 2015 by Edizioni Ca'Foscari and in 2019 by Asterios.

The chapters that constitute the *second part* of the book (chapters 5 to 9) present new empirical and analytical elements necessary to comprehend the world of work in contemporary capitalism, seeking to show the validity of the core formulations presented in *Adeus ao Trabalho?*. In this sense, our hope is to contribute to understand the crucial topic of *work*, which alongside the *ecological* question is part of the vital issues of our time.

If in the recent past these tendencies seemed to affect *only* countries in the Global South, the expansion of neoliberalism and the financialization of the economy, in a context of a deep *structural crisis of capital* (which from 2008 became more acute) show that this destructive movement is increasing also in the Global North, trying to destroy what was built throughout the long 20th century through many struggles of the working class.

∴

I would like to say here a special thank you to my friend professor Ricardo Rezende for his splendid illustration on the cover of this book; and another thank you, also special, goes to Labour Public Prosecutor Renata Coelho, for all her support to our research.

About *Farewell to Work?*

Ricardo Antunes is a lucid and passionate (these two characteristics can coincide) narrator of the epochal transformations of workers' labouring, living and organisational conditions [...] A narrator that, in profoundly describing the capacity of global capital to materially transform and subjectively manipulate work and workers, never loses sight of society's social antagonisms and of the possibilities of emancipation from wage labour, inscribed in the capitalist social relations of our time.
— *Pietro Basso, Un cataclisma, e il suo lucido narratore. Preface to the Italian edition of Farewell to Work?*

Ricardo Antunes's book presents theoretical insights of great interest on the current question of the Marxist distinction between 'abstract labour' and 'concrete labour', and on the increasing hegemony of the former on the latter, under the capitalist organization of society. Supported by György Lukács' Ontology of Social Being, this Brazilian sociologist courageously defends the idea of labour's central role as the 'proto-form' of social organization, and clarifies the importance of the transition from the heteronomous condition of workers to that of real autonomy.
— *Nicolas Tertulian, Actuel Marx no. 22, France*

I have read Farewell to Work? with all the attention that it deserves. The question of changes in the organic composition of capital – with all its justified controversies – is really a matter of concern to all of us. I dealt with this problem, a long time ago, when I had the energy for such a task. In almost all of the Western languages, there is an extensive bibliography on the subject. Behind it lies the peculiar idea that the category of labour is vanishing. This is similar to that theoretical current that longs for a society in which only the bourgeoisie exists, without the proletariat. I really like this book. It is clear, objective, well-informed and indispensable to those worried by the subject. Congratulations! It is the most important book on Economy and Politics that has emerged here in the last years, very long years.
— *Nelson Werneck Sodré, Brazilian historian*

This remarkable and very up-to-date book by Ricardo Antunes demonstrates that capitalism, above all, remains a form of exploiting the workforce. Technical and social forms of organizing the production of commodities – whether material or cultural, prosaic or virtual – are modified. It is not about waving "farewell to work", but to recognize along with Ricardo Antunes that forms of labour and production's technical and social organisation change continuously, nationwide and worldwide. In all cases, the expropriation is put in question, always accompanied by the contradictions between labour and capital, i.e., the workers and the owners of the means of production. That is why the class contradictions remain the main driver in the history of capitalism, moving towards socialism.

— *Octávio Ianni, from the back cover of the Spanish edition of Farewell to Work?*

Acknowledgements

For his help with the English version of *Farewell to Work?* I would like to thank Murillo van der Laan. In addition to translating the first part of the book, he was working with me as an assistant editor/curator. During the preparation of this volume, he helped select the texts that were included in the second part of the book, he rationalized the technical translations into English categories, concepts, quotations, and etc. In addition, he standardized references and expressions used in the text, formatted the manuscript following the publisher guidelines and helped oversee the final details required to facilitate publication of *Farewell to Work?*

Tables

1   Oscillations in labour power in United States (1980–1986)   25
2   Unionization Rates, 1988   38

Introduction

In 1980, André Gorz published his well-known book *Farewell to the Working Class*. Assertive – capturing a developing trend showing a meaningful reduction of industrial workers in advanced-capitalist societies – the French sociologist *predicted the end of the working class*, with all the *theoretical and political* consequences of this formulation.

The book had an unusual repercussion, not only in the universe (academic and political) of capitalist core countries – which were experiencing more intensively the empirical trends that Gorz was trying to capture – but also in countries of medium-scale industrialization, like Brazil, which were in the *counterflow of the European scenario*, witnessing a strong resurgence of *its* workers movement. A very thought-provoking and a highly problematic essay, *Farewell to the Working Class* tried to question labour revolution at its roots; therefore, it helped to further disorient the traditional left.

If one of its objectives were to put the debate on a new level, it can be said that *Farewell to the Working Class* was, *in this sense*, a successful book. It was followed by several texts that had formulations which, directly or indirectly, approved or rejected André Gorz's thesis. To mention some of those texts, we can recall books or articles (for sure, very distinct and heterogenous) from Claus Offe, Benjamin Coriat, Alain Touraine, Jean Lojkine, Fergus Murray, Adam Schaff, Ernest Mandel, István Mészáros, Robert Kurz, Alain Bihr, Thomas Gounet, Frank Annunziato, David Harvey, Simon Clarke, and many others, who addressed problems related to the present and the future of the world of work.

This was the controversy that directly inspired this essay, entitled *Farewell to Work? (Essays on the World of Work's Metamorphoses and Centrality)*, whose goal is an *attempt to offer* some basic elements and outlines of this debate – from a perspective situated in this particular corner of a world marked by an *unevenly articulated globalization*.

The questions we pursued are essentially these: is the *class-that-lives-from-labour disappearing*? Does *the retraction of the traditional Fordist industrial worker inevitably result in a loss of reference* for *the labouring social being*? Which repercussions did these metamorphoses have (and does has) in the institutions that represent workers, of which unions are an expression? And as an analytical derivation of the ongoing transformations, it seems inevitable to ask the following: is the category labour still central *in contemporary society's universe of human praxis*? Should the *so-called 'crisis of labouring society'* be understood as *the end of the possibility of a labour revolution*? Is labour no longer *the structuring element of a new form of human sociability*? Is it no longer the proto-form *of human activity, which operates the metabolic relationship between humans and nature?*

These are deep questions and this text intends to offer only *some direction* on them. In a historical moment marked by several transformations, many of them still happening, we think an intervention in this debate, in the form of an essay, has a *preliminary and limited character*.

Farewell to Work? is part of broader volume of work: the Habilitation thesis in Sociology of Work I presented, in April 1994, to the Department of Sociology at the Institute of Philosophy and Human Sciences at the University of Campinas (Unicamp). It was appraised by professors Octávio Ianni, Maurício Tragtenberg, Paulo Silveira, Sedi Hirano and Celso Frederico. From them, I received several suggestions and some direction. The book is also part of a research project that we are currently developing with the support of the *National Council for Scientific and Technological Development* (CNPq), entitled *Where is the World of Work heading to?*, in which we try to apprehend the working class' *form of being* in the contemporary society. This essay is a first result of those investigations.

Complementing this volume, as an appendix, are texts addressing some points or questions raised in *Farewell to Work?*. The 'common thread' amongst them are issues related to the crisis of the labour society.

I would like to finish the introduction to this essay, which deals with the dilemmas and controversies around a *meaningful life in and from work*, trying to express the feeling generated by intellectual work. Goethe once said:

> If you inquire what the people are like here, I must answer, 'The same as everywhere.' The human race is but a monotonous affair. Most of them labour the greater part of their time for mere subsistence; and the scanty portion of freedom which remains to them so troubles them that they use every exertion to get rid of it. Oh, the destiny of man!' (Werther).

Intellectual work, in its deep and true meaning, is *one* of the rare moments opposed to this 'monotonous affair'.

I would like to express here my sincere gratitude to the students of the research line *Labour and Trade Unionism* from the *Social Sciences Post-Graduate Program* of Unicamp. For some years now I have been discussing with them many of the ideas in this book. Without this constant and fruitful dialogue, this text certainly would not have taken the form that it has.

PART 1

Heterogeneity and Fragmentation of the Working Class

∴

CHAPTER 1

Fordism, Toyotism and Flexible Accumulation

During the 1980s, core capitalist countries experienced deep transformations in their world of work. The changes in the latter forms of insertion in the productive structure, in its forms of representation in trade unions and in its politics were so intense that it is possible to claim that the *class-that-lives-from-labour* suffered its most acute crisis in this century. It hit not only the world of work's *materiality*, but resonated deeply in its *subjectivity* and, in the close interrelation between these two levels, the crisis impacted its *form of being*.

This text intends to develop some points in the debate around the dimensions and meanings of these changes and some of its possible and visible consequences (theoretical and empirical). It cannot, therefore, have a conclusive position, but aims to present some indications that could offer some answers to the many contemporary questions.

Let's start listing some of the changes and transformations during the 1980s. In a decade of large technological leaps, factories were invaded by automation, robotics and microelectronics, which inserted and developed themselves into labour relations and capital production. A number of experiments – more or less: intense, consolidated, trending and embryonic – took place in production. Fordism and Taylorism are no longer the sole production processes, mixing with other processes (neo-fordism, neo-taylorism, post-fordism) that resulted from the experiences of the 'Third Italy', and the following regions: Sweden (in the Kalmar region, originating 'kalmarism'), Silicon Valley, and some regions in Germany, among others. In some cases, Fordism and Taylorism have been completely replaced, as shown by the Japanese experience of Toyotism.

New production processes emerged where the *chronometer* and *serial massive production* were 'replaced' by the flexibilization of production, 'flexible specialization', new patterns of seeking productivity, new forms to adapt production to the logic of the market.[1] New ways to deconcentrate industries were

---

1   Fergus Murray, "The Decentralization of Production – The Decline of the Mass-Collective Worker", *Capital & Class,* no. 19 (1983); Charles Sabel & Michael Piore, *The Second Industrial Divide: Possibilities for Prosperity* (New York: Basic Books, 1984); Frank Annunziato, "Il Fordismo nella Critica di Gramsci e nella Realtà Statunitense Contemporanea", *Critica Marxista,* no. 6 (1989); Simon Clarke, "The Crisis of Fordism or the Crisis of Social-Democracy?", *Telos,* no. 83 (1990); Thomas Gounet, "Luttes Concurrentielles et Stratégies d'Accumulation dans l'Industries Automobile", *Études Marxistes,* no. 10 (1991); "Penser à l'Envers ... Le Capitalisme", *Études Marxistes,* no. 14 (1992); David Harvey, *The Condition of Postmodernity: An Enquiry into the*

tested and new patterns to manage the labour power were pursued. Quality Control Circles, 'participatory management' and the search for 'total quality' are visible expressions of this, not only in the Japanese world, but also in several core capitalist countries and in the industrialized periphery. Toyotism penetrates, mixes itself into or even replaces the dominant Fordist standard in different parts of globalized capitalism. Transitory forms of production were experienced and the impact was acute also on labour rights. They were deregulated, made flexible, in a way to give capital the necessary tools to adapt to its new stage. Historically hard-won labour rights and benefits were replaced and eliminated from the world of production. Taylorist despotism was reduced or mixed – depending on its strength – with participation inside the company's order and universe, using the manipulative engagement typical of sociability shaped by the contemporary commodity-producing system.

This is not the place for a detailed analysis of this current process. We would like to highlight, nevertheless, some of the elements we consider most relevant, to later point out the repercussions that these transformations had in the world of work.

Initially, we reaffirm that we understand Fordism *fundamentally* as the form in which manufacturing and the labour process consolidated themselves in this century. Its basic constitutive elements were: mass production, put forward by the assembly line of more homogeneous products; control of timing and movements with the Taylorist chronometer and Fordist serial production; separation between conception and execution in the labour process; concentration and vertical organization of manufacturing units; and the constitution/consolidation of the *mass-worker*, the collective industrial worker, etc.

Less than a model to organize society, extending itself also to different social spheres, we understand Fordism rather as a labour process that, along with Taylorism, predominated in large capitalist industry in this century.

Sabel and Piore's work is considered ground-breaking in presenting the thesis of *'flexible specialization'*. The latter would be an expression of a process that made possible the emergence of a *new productive form* – 'Third Italy', particularly, being the concrete experience. This *new productive form* articulates, on one side, significant technological development and, on the other, productive deconcentration based on medium and small 'artisan' companies. As it expanded and generalized itself, this symbiosis overcame the hitherto

---

Origins of Cultural Change (Oxford: Blackwell Publishers, 1990); Benjamin Coriat, *El Taller y el Robot: Ensayos Sobre el Fordismo y la Producción en Masa en la Era de la Electrónica* (Ciudad de México: Siglo XXI, 1992); *Pensar al Revés: Trabajo y Organización en la Empresa Japonesa* (Ciudad de México: Siglo XXI, 1992).

predominant Fordist pattern. The new productive paradigm also expressed, according to Sabel and Piore, a model that refused *mass production* typical of Fordist *large industry*, and reclaimed a conception of labour which, being more flexible, was exempt from the *alienation* inherent in Fordist accumulation. An 'artisan' process, more deconcentrated and technologically developed, producing for a more regional market, extinguishing *serial* production and inspired by Neo-proudhonism; this would be the production model responsible for overcoming what, until recently, dominated capitalist production – with successful experiences in the United States, Germany and France, among other countries. The excess of Fordism and mass production, detrimental to labour and suppressing its creativity, would be the causal element of capitalist crisis.[2]

Many criticized Piore and Sabel showing, on one side, the impossibility of generalizing this model, and on the other, the *epidermal* meaning of these changes. Coriat, for instance, claims that the implicit hypothesis in this thesis, the replacement of a production based in an *economy of scale*, is empirically unattainable. Since the exclusive feature of *flexible specialization* is supported by essentially segmented and unstable markets, it is hard to imagine its generalization. Coriat, therefore, speaks of an 'abusive generalization' in Sabel and Piore's *flexible specialization* thesis.[3]

Clarke's critique is sharper. Drawing on arguments from other authors, he claims that the original thesis of *flexible specialization* is not 'universally applicable', it is incoherent in various aspects and it is not empirically sustainable when pointing to: the overcome of *mass market*, the inability of this kind of production to adapt to economic changes and the "claimed correlation between new technology and the scale and social forms of production". Clarke reasserts the theory that *flexible specialization* resulted in labour intensification and it is a way to deskill and disorganize workers.[4] His proposition, nevertheless, is more polemic and even problematic when claiming that Fordism has a *flexible* dimension, capable of assimilating all ongoing transformations into its logic: "[...] the principles of Fordism have proved applicable in an extraordinarily wide range of technical contexts".[5]

Clarke advances an *extended* conception of Fordism, understanding it as not limited to technological and industrial dimensions, but as also comprising social relations of production. He does not see the contemporary capital's reproduction crisis as a *post-fordist restructuring* and says

---

2 Sabel & Piore, *The Second Industrial Divide*.
3 Coriat, *El Taller y el Robot*, 151–153.
4 Clarke, "The Crisis of Fordism", 77–78.
5 Ibid., 80.

[...] just as competitive pressures from new, more highly developed and more flexible forms of Fordism soon forced Ford to introduce Pinkerton's men and the Service Department, so the flexible specialists and niche marketeers are already coming under pressure from competitors who have managed to reconcile economies of scope with economies of scale.

Clark, then, concludes that 'the crisis of Fordism is nothing new; it is only the latest manifestation of the permanent crisis of capitalism'.[6]

Frank Annunziato also indicates some critical problems on the position that defends positiveness and enhancement in *flexible specialization*. He shows that Piore and Sabel understand artisan production as a necessary path to preserve capitalism and contests the authors' conception of 'yeoman democracy'. As Annunziato argues, Fordism still dominates the United States' economy, since the latter has a taylorized labour process and capitalism's hegemony penetrates workers' organizations, either trade unions or political parties.[7]

It is important to also mention Fergus Murray's comments in a text published in 1983 – in the early stages of the debate. There he shows that, in the last decade, the trend to decentralize production hit a group of companies, in Italy, which reduced the size of their industrial plants and encouraged *putting-out systems* of work, pointing in the direction of small units of artisan production, *domestic outworkers*. Similar processes are taking place in Japan, raising the productivity of small companies through technological development and using computer systems to articulate them to large conglomerates. Changes, with certain similarities, are also happening in Southern United States and in Great Britain (Wales and Scotland). Murray also refers to the ongoing reduction of General Electric's industrial plants. His text addresses the evidence challenging the thesis that progressive centralization and concentration of capital necessarily result in physical concentration of the space of production. For Murray, historical and specific conditions can make it possible the emergence of these small production units – as in the Italian case. Among the most important elements that define an industrial plant, he lists the kind of product, the existing technological alternatives, the control of the production processes, the industrial relations and the law.[8]

Murray also shows how the articulation between *decentralization of production* and *technological development,* particularly in the Italian case – which

---

6　Ibid., 90.
7　Annunziato, "Il Fordismo nella Critica di Gramsci", 99–100; 106.
8　Murray, "The Decentralization of Production", 79–85.

is the empirical basis of his research – has the clear goal of confronting the autonomy and cohesion of Italian workers, to the point that Murray suggests a necessary reconsideration of the role played by the *collective mass worker*, given that it is not as strong as it was in 1960s and 1970s. The text defines several forms of production decentralization, showing that fragmentation of labour, alongside technological development, can increase capital's exploitation and control of the labour power. It also shows how Italian unions, which developed in the universe of the *mass collective worker*, found it difficult to assimilate and incorporate this more segmented working class.[9]

David Harvey offers a suggestive analytical attempt to apprehend the meaning and outlines of capitalist transformations. He understands that the essential features of Fordism, based on *mass* production, were strong until at least 1973. In his analysis, the working class' living standards of core capitalist countries maintained a relative stability, as did the monopolistic profits. After the sharp recession that began in 1973, a transition started in the process of capital accumulation.

In his synthesis of *flexible accumulation*, Harvey says that this stage of production is

> marked by a direct confrontation with the rigidities of Fordism. It relies on flexibility with respect to labour processes, labour markets, products, and patterns of consumption. It is characterized by the emergence of entirely new sectors of production, new ways of providing financial services, new markets, and, above all, greatly intensified rates of commercial, technological, and organizational innovation. It has entrained rapid shifts in the patterning of uneven development, both between sectors and between geographical regions, giving rise, for example, to a vast surge in so-called 'service-sector' employment as well as to entirely new industrial ensembles in hitherto underdeveloped regions.[10]

Although Harvey claims that companies based on the Fordist model could adopt new technologies and the emerging labour processes (what is often called neo-Fordism), he recognizes, nevertheless, that competitive pressures, as well as the struggle to control the labour power, resulted in

---

9   Ibid., 79–99.
10 Harvey, *The Condition of Postmodernity*, 147.

entirely new industrial forms or to the integration of Fordism with a whole network of sub-contracting and 'outsourcing' to give greater flexibility in the face of heightened competition and greater risk.[11]

Distancing himself from either those who talk about '*new production processes*', entirely different from a Fordist basis (as do Sabel and Piore[12]), or those who do not see new or meaningful transformations in the process of capital production; Harvey recognizes the existence of a combination of production processes, which articulates Fordism with flexible, 'artisan', traditional processes. According to him,

> the insistence that there is nothing essentially new in the push towards flexibility, and that capitalism has periodically taken these sorts of paths before, is certainly correct (a careful reading of Marx's *Capital* sustains the point). The argument that there is an acute danger of exaggerating the significance of any trend towards increased flexibility and geographical mobility, blinding us to how strongly implanted Fordist production systems still are, deserves careful consideration. And the ideological and political consequences of overemphasizing flexibility in the narrow sense of production technique and labour relations are serious enough to make sober and careful evaluations of the degree of flexibility imperative [...] But I think it equally dangerous to pretend that nothing has changed, when the facts of deindustrialization and of plant relocation, of more flexible manning practices and labour markets, of automation and product innovation, stare most workers in the face.[13]

As a consequence of these formulations, Harvey develops his thesis that flexible accumulation, in the *sense that it still is a particular form of capitalism* preserves three essential features of this mode of production. *First*, it is focused on growth; *second*, this growth, in real values, is based on exploitation of living labour in the universe of production; and *third*, capitalism has an intrinsic technological and organizational dynamic. Particularly, about the second feature Harvey adds:

> interestingly, the deployment of new technologies has so freed surpluses of labour power as to make the revival of absolute strategies for procuring

---

11   Ibid., 155–156.
12   Sabel & Piore, *The Second Industrial Divide*.
13   Harvey, *The Condition of Postmodernity*, 191.

surplus value more feasible even in the advanced capitalist countries [...] the revival of the sweatshops in New York and Los Angeles, of home work and 'telecommuting', as well as the burgeoning growth of informal sector labour practices throughout the advanced capitalist world, does indeed represent a rather sobering vision of capitalism's supposedly progressive history. Under conditions of flexible accumulation, it seems as if alternative labour systems can exist side by side within the same space in such a way as to enable capitalist entrepreneurs to choose at will between them. The same shirt designs can be produced by large-scale factories in India, co-operative production in 'Third Italy', sweatshops in New York and London, or family labour systems in Hong Kong.[14]

The consequence of this process, when it concerns the world of work, was also indicated by Harvey: organized workers were undermined. Results were seen in high levels of structural unemployment and in the regression of trade union action. Among many other negative consequences, rampant individualism, in particular, thrived.[15]

If these experiences of flexible accumulation, based in 'Third Italy' and other places like Sweden,[16] brought many consequences in very different

14   Ibid., 187.
15   Ibid.
16   Among the various experiences of production flexibilization, Gorz mentions the operation of Volvo in Uddevalla, Sweden: "workers in this plant are organized in teams of ten peoples, men and women, and each team ensures the complete assemblage and finishing tasks of a vehicle. Each worker knows several crafts and the different functions rotate among them, including management. Members of the team can organize among themselves supplemental breaks, taken by turns; and the plan, which normally is 10 vehicles by team per week, can be fulfilled in a very flexible way: the volume of production can vary during the days and even the weeks, but the weekly average of 12 cars is maintained [...] The plant in Uddevalla is an assemblage and finishing factory. Workers can feel responsible for the quality of the assemblage, but neither the quality of the elements and groups, nor the conception of the vehicles, nor the decision to produce cars depend on them. Therefore, their labour's final product continues to be – in a great part – alienated, as is also alien to the workers who control the robotized production of motors, gearboxes, supports, etc. [...] Even when they access high degrees of autonomy, of sovereignty in work, they remain alienated because they do not have the possibility to control, establish and self-determine the goals of their activities. They remain servicing objectives they cannot choose, of which, in most cases, they are not even aware of". See André Gorz, "O Futuro da Classe Operária", *Revista Internacional, Quinzena*, no. 101 (1990). About the Swedish experience, see also Christian Berggren, "New Production Concepts in Final Assembly: The Swedish Experience", in *The Transformation of Work: skill, flexibility, and the labour process*, ed. Stephen Wood (London: Unwin Hyman, 1989), 171–203.

directions, it is *Toyotism or the Japanese model*, however, that has been causing a larger impact. Either by its technical revolution in Japanese industry or by the potential to spread *some of its basic features*, Toyotism had such an expansion that nowadays reaches a world scale.

It is not our goal here to analyse in details the steps that singularize the experience of Toyotism (or *Ohnism*, from Ohno, the engineer who created Toyota's model), not even in its most universalizing dimensions, which gave it an extraordinary impact as an agile and profitable process of commodity production. What we intend is to offer some of the constitutive features of this new model and point to some of the vast consequences it has in the world of work.

Coriat talks about four stages resulting in the emergence of *Toyotism*. *First* is the introduction in the Japanese car industry of experiences from the textile sector in which workers need to operate several machines simultaneously. *Second,* the companies' need to respond to financial crises, increasing production without increasing the number of workers. *Third* is the importation of management techniques from American supermarkets, which ultimately resulted in the emergence of *Kanban*. According to Toyoda, president and founder of Toyota, "the ideal is to produce only what is needed and in the best time", mirroring supermarkets' model, which refill products only after they were sold. Coriat says the *Kanban* method existed in a generalized way and in essential sections of Toyota since 1962, although *Toyotism*, as a more general model, originated after the *Second World War. Fourth stage* is the expansion of the *Kanban* method to subcontracted companies and suppliers.[17]

Coriat also mentions another meaningful feature of *Toyotism,* the need to respond to an internal market demanding distinguished products and characterized by small orders, which were a result of the limited conditions of postwar Japan. In Coriat's words,

> in these conditions, competence and competitivity were determined by *the capacity to rapidly satisfy small and varied orders*. In this context, therefore, Ohnism emerged: in the universe of unique and original pressures, when compared to the ones from which Fordism arose.[18]

It was also necessary to overcome the chaotic character of Toyota's production, facetiously called the DEKANSCHO method – which referred to a long period

---

17   Coriat, *Pensar al Revés*, 27–30.
18   Ibid., 33–34.

of preparation before production, similar to philosophy students that slept a whole semester before intensively study Descartes, Kant and Schopenhauer. As an example of this limitation in production it suffices to mention that, in 1955, the Japanese car industry produced 69,000 unities, while the United States produced 9.2 million, Germany 909,000, and France 725,000.[19]

Finally, there was also the need to confront Japanese trade unions, with their history of strikes and confrontation, which constituted a barrier to the expansion of Toyotism. In 1950, there were important strikes against massive dismissals in Toyota (between 1,600 and 2,000 workers). The long metalworkers' strike was defeated by the company. In this new context, it was the first defeat of Japan's very militant trade unions. In 1952/1953, new struggles emerged in several companies for wage increases and against the rationalisation of labour. It lasted 55 days, but trade unions were once again defeated.[20] It is important to remember that Nissan, in this conflict, used *lockout* as a way to demoralize the strike.[21] After repression of the main trade unions' leaders, companies took advantage of the disorganization of militant trade unions and created what constituted the *distinctive feature of Japanese trade unions in the Toyotist period: enterprise trade unionism, the house union*, bonded to the employer's ideas and universe. In the following year, 1954, this same trade union was considered not collaborative enough and was, therefore, dissolved and replaced by a new trade union integrated into the 'Toyota Spirit' or 'Toyota Family'. The trade union campaign, in that year, was run under the new banner, 'protect our company to defend life! [...]'.[22] *This was an essential condition for the capitalist success of the Japanese companies* and, in particular, for Toyota. Combining repression with assimilation, *enterprise unionism* gained, as compensation for its subordination, lifetime job for some of the workers in large companies (around 30% of working population) and also monetary benefits linked to productivity. As it happens in Nissan, unions have an important role in the firms' 'meritocracy', since they have a say in the promotion of workers (with the possibility of veto).[23] Coriat says, referring also to Japanese trade unionism, that in several situations, taking on a place in unions is a condition to be promoted to positions of responsibility in the company, especially in human management – which bonds unions tight to the businesses' hierarchies.[24]

---

19   Ibid., 31; 35.
20   Ibid., 36; Gounet, "Luttes Concurrentielles", 42.
21   Ibid., 42.
22   Coriat, *Pensar al Revés*, 37.
23   Gounet, "Penser à l'Envers", 67.
24   Coriat, *Pensar al Revés*, 70.

It seems unnecessary to recall that these practices subordinate workers to the companies' universe, creating conditions for the emergence of an enduring *involvement trade unionism*, essentially *manipulated* and *assimilated*.[25] It was in these historical conditions that the Japanese model – which we are calling here *Toyotism* – was conceived.

Its basic constitutive features can be summarized by the following: different from Fordism, Toyotist production is directly led by demand; it is diversified and ready to attend consumption. It is the latter that determines what will be produced, the opposite of what happens in Fordist *serial and massive* production. Toyotism is based on the existence of a *minimal stock*. The best use of production time – including transport, quality control and stock handling – is guaranteed by the *just in time* methods. The *Kanban*, or the card used to indicate the need to refill production parts, is essential since the process is inverted: it is at the end, after the sale, that restocking starts and *Kanban* is the sign used to show the need to refill parts/products. This is why *Kanban* is associated with the way supermarkets work, since they fill-up shelves with products after sales occur.[26]

To respond to the more individualized demands from the market, in the best timing and with the best 'quality', it is necessary that production be based on a flexible production process, which allows one worker to operate several machines (an average of five machines at Toyota), breaking with the one-person/one-machine relation in Fordism. The so-called 'polyvalence' of the Japanese worker, more than an expression and an example of greater

---

25 This differs from Coriat's interpretation, which sees in this relation between unions and companies "a game of subtle and essential compensations". "It is a *set of implicit and explicit compensations* given to unions and big companies' workers 'in exchange' to their commitment with production". *Cooperative unionism* "has historically shown to be capable to ensure continuous and substantial improvements to the living condition of wage-workers". See *Pensar al Revés*, 37–38; 71. Gounet makes an acute critique of Coriat's thesis (and also Lipietz's) in his long essay *Penser à L'enver ... le capitalisme*, *Études Marxistes*, no. 14, may 1992, Belgium (a special issue dedicated to Toyotism). Frank Annunziato suggestively alludes to the Japanese particular relation between labour and capital: "the Japanese Capitalist, as an incarnation of a feudal lord, guarantees labour's stability, getting from workers, in exchange, as incarnations of feudal serfs, loyalty and obedience". See Annunziato, "Il Fordismo nella Critica di Gramsci", 113. If this is a strong tendency in parts of the Japanese working class, it is important to remember that there is resistance in segments of workers and unions: "until recently, unions worked in the same perspective of the companies. As they were not heard about decisions to transfer factories to other countries, unions started to oppose, at least verbally, to companies' policies, since they understand that this jeopardizes the right to stability". See Ben Watanabe, "Toyotismo: Um Novo Padrão Mundial de Produção?", *Revista dos Metalúrgicos*, December 1993, 13.

26 Gounet, "Penser à l'Envers", 40; Coriat, *Pensar al Revés*, 43–45.

skills, shows the capacity of a worker to operate several machines, combining 'various simple tasks' (as shows the interesting testimony of Ken Watanabe, a former union leader).[27] Coriat speaks of a *de-specialization and polyvalence* of skilled professional workers, making them *multifunctional workers*.[28]

In a similar vein, work is now done by teams, breaking with the typical Fordist form of production.[29] A team of workers operates a system of automated machines. Besides flexibility of the production apparatus, there is also the need to render the organisation of labour flexible. It is also necessary to rapidly adapt machines and tools to produce new commodities. On this point, there is a clear difference from Fordist rigidity. Gounet says that this is one of the greatest obstacles to a wider expansion of Toyotism that could transform the production structures already in place, which resists flexibilization. Unlike Fordism verticalization, exemplified by American factories where there was a *vertical integration* when automakers widened their production areas, in Toyotism there is a *horizontalization* that reduces the production sphere of the company and outsources the manufacturing of basic elements to other firms, which in Fordism were integrated into the main company. This horizontal approach also results in the extension of Toyotist methods to the whole network of suppliers. In this sense, *kanban, just in time*, flexibilization, outsourcing, subcontracting, Quality Control Circles, total quality control, elimination of waste, participatory management, enterprise trade unionism, among many other elements are propagated intensively.

Gounet also shows that the Toyotist system presupposes an intensification of labour exploitation, both by the fact that workers operate simultaneously with several different machines and by the fact that capital uses a light system (green = everything is working normally; orange = maximum intensity; red = production problems) to intensify – without suffocating – labour's productive rhythm. Lights must always change between green and orange to reach an intense rhythm of labour and production. The reduction of 'porosity' in work is even greater than in Fordism. This feature of Toyotism is used by Gounet in an acute critique of Coriat, who acknowledges that the light system grants a better control of workers by management, but overlooks what is central: the method serves to continuously accelerate the production chain's speed. The constant oscillation between green and orange allows the management to detect problems in advance and suppress them in a way to speed up the pace until the next problem or difficulty emerges.[30]

---

27   Watanabe, "Toyotismo", 9.
28   Coriat, *Pensar al Revés.*, 41.
29   Gounet, "Penser à l'Envers", 40.
30   Ibid., 66.

Another essential point of Toyotism is that for an effective flexibilization of the production apparatus, flexibilization of workers is also crucial. Flexible rights are needed in order for labour power be used directly according to the consumer market's need. Toyotism structures itself on a minimum number of workers, extending this amount through overtime, temporary workers and sub-contracting, depending on market conditions. The basic starting point is a reduced number of workers and the undertaking of overtime. This explains why a Toyota worker labours approximately an average of 2,300 hours per year, while a Belgian (Ford-Genk, General Motors-Anvers, Volkswagen-Forest, Renault Vilvoverde and Volvo-Grand) worker labours between 1,550 and 1,650 hours per year (data from ABVVLIMBUG, Belgium, June 1990).[31] Another expression of the Japanese model is stamped in comparative data gathered by the *Massachusetts Institute of Technology*, which in 1987 estimated the number of hours per worker to make a vehicle:

> 19 hours in the Archipelago; 26.5 hours, on average, in the United States; 22.6 hours in the best European factories and 35.6 hours, on average, in Europe, almost twice as much than in the Far East.[32]

Gounet then synthesizes that:

> Toyotism is an answer to the 1970s Fordist crisis. In the place of deskilled labour, the worker becomes now polyvalent. Instead of the individualized line, he is integrated into a team. Rather than producing mass vehicles for people he does not know, he makes an element to 'satisfy' the team located in the sequence of his line.

And he concludes, not without a stroke of irony:

> In sum, with Toyotism it seems to disappear the repetitive, ultra-simple, demotivating and brutish labour. Finally, we are in the stage of enriching tasks, of consumer's satisfaction, of quality control.[33]

The testimony from Ben Watanabe – a 30-year activist in Japanese labour unions – is suggestive:

---

31 Mentioned in Gounet, "Luttes Concurrentielles", 41.
32 Krafick quoted in Gounet, "Luttes Concurrentielles", 42; 50.
33 Ibid., 43.

the QCC was developed in Japan by managers, from 1950s onwards, alongside Toyotism. In Toyota's system, engineers at the shop floor no longer have a strategic role and production is controlled by a group of workers. The company invests heavily in training, participation and suggestions to improve quality and productivity. Quality control is only one part of QCC.

In this, nevertheless, "is included another element: the abolition of workers' independent organization".[34]

> Toyota works with groups of 8 workers [...] If only one of them fails, the group loses its pay raise. So, the group guarantees productivity, assuming a role formerly assigned to management. The same kind of control deals with absenteeism.[35]

On the diversity of trade unions in Japan, Watanabe adds that at the top of the pyramid there are unions by companies, with high rates of unionisation, "but at the lowest levels, workers are barely organized: the number of unionised is not above 5% of the total".[36] This diversity was pointed out also by Coriat, referring to the formulation of another author:

> trade unions in Japan, although dominated by the company union type, must be understood as a *continuum*, which stretches from highly bureaucratic ones, organizing hundreds of thousands of wageworkers, to the 'association' in a small business, which occasionally becomes a collective negotiator.[37]

As for lifetime jobs, Watanabe's testimony is once again interesting. He says that this system

> began in 1961. To commit workers to increase quality and productivity, business owners offered this benefit. In the beginning, no one believed in stability, which was implemented, in fact, in 1965. Nevertheless, this practice was adopted by large companies, reaching, approximately, 30% of Japanese workers.[38]

---

34 Watanabe, "Toyotismo", 5.
35 Ibid.
36 Ibid., 8.
37 Nohara quoted in Coriat, *Pensar al Revés*, 71.
38 Watanabe, "Toyotismo", 10–11.

Watanabe adds that this experience

> is very short and, nowadays, is facing a possible crisis. Economic recession, which began 2 years ago, pushed the National Organization of Companies to suggest managers rethink lifetime stability for the next negotiation. It is necessary to also remember that lifetime jobs are closely linked to wage structure, which correspond to the need companies had in the 1950s, at the initial stage of Toyotism's development, to guarantee that workers stayed in the same factory.
>
> Retired at 55 years old, the worker is then transferred to a job that pay less in smaller companies with less prestige.[39]

There is also, in the universe of a lifetime job, with all the singularities of the Japanese model – and its large limitations – another outcome from the labour conditions in the Archipelago: the *karoshi*, the *sudden death at work* caused by the rhythm and intensity of the relentless search to increase productivity.[40]

If these are the model's basic outlines in Japanese concreteness, where it was created and developed, its expansion worldwide, in less 'pure' and more hybrid forms, has also been staggering. With the exception of the lifetime job, the Japanese model, in one way or other, more or less 'adapted', more or less distinguished, has shown great potential to universalize, with negative consequences to the world of work, in Western European countries, and on the American continent (North and South) – not to mention, naturally, the recent 'Asian Tigers', which expanded themselves after the Japanese model.

Coriat suggests that, in an internationalized universe, if the 'lessons' from Japan are copied everywhere this is because it matches the current stage of capitalism, marked by increased competition, diversification and quality – original conditions that constituted the *Ohnian* method. Since Coriat adds that "not everything is negative" and that one should not "think of reversing" the Japanese model, his proposal goes towards integrating, *under a social-democratic version*, "all democracy into labour relations", grounded in "renewed and much more solid and dynamic bases, which will be capable of combining economic efficiency and equity".[41] The contradictions and paradoxes that Coriat presents are secondary or even phenomenic, because they are embedded in a positive outlook that predominates in his analysis of Toyotism. The critical features he

---

39   Ibid., 4–11. See also Ben Watanabe, "Karoshi, Made in Japan", *Revista Internacional, Quinzena*, no. 167 (1993), 3.
40   Ibid., 30.
41   Coriat, *Pensar al Revés*, 146–147.

presents are diluted and overlapped by the advantages of the Japanese model. Coriat's conclusion is clear: "to western companies, the challenge – in truth, the only one – consists [...] in passing from incited engagement to negotiated engagement [...]". Therefore,

> the already old practice of co-determination, in its German or Swedish form, in more than one aspect has known how to open itself to these new dynamics 'of the Japanese type', in which new skills, training and internal markets are systematically built as the base of productivity and quality [...] It would be the ultimate paradox – in truth, a magnificent one –, if the Japanese lesson, 'transferring' itself to old Europe, could finally translate into a wider [...] democracy.[42]

We believe, conversely, that the introduction and expansion of Toyotism in 'old Europe' will tend to further undermine what was possible to preserve from the welfare state, since the Japanese model is much more in line with the neoliberal logic than with a truly social-democratic conception. The greater risk we see in this *westernization* of Toyotism is that, with the retraction of European social-democratic governments, as well as their subordination to several points of the neoliberal agenda, there would be a greater shrinkage in public funds, resulting in a further reduction of the social gains available for the *entire* population, both for the part of the population that works and those who cannot find a job.

It is not difficult to conclude that the 'Japanese advantage' – given by 'wage gains resulting from productivity' – which benefits a minority of the Japanese working class,[43] would take place further undermining the conditions of the working population that depends on public funds. Less than a

---

42   Ibid., 156–157.
43   See Watanabe's testimony: "although they receive the car industry world's highest wages (measured in dollars), Japanese workers cannot buy a decent house without a loan. It is the companies that, after a certain period of work (between 10 and 15 years), offer low interest loans, which also bonds the worker to the company". Watanabe, "Toyotismo", 11. Japanese conditions, considering the working class as a whole, are described by Robert Kurz as following: "in this regard, Japan distinguishes itself from Western conditions because it never effectively managed to overcame its Third World internal structures. The poverty among their elders is part of a brutality not known in Europe; the wages and living standards of the mass of workers employed in the industries that supplies multinationals are often inhumane; and the infrastructure is at the level of 1950s Europe; apartments without toilets, and latrines in the courtyards are the rule and not the exception [...]". Robert Kurz, *O Colapso da Modernização: Da Derrocada do Socialismo de Caserna à Crise da Economia Mundial* (São Paulo: Paz e Terra, 1992), 148.

social-democratization of Toyotism, we would have a *toyotization* that would mischaracterize and disorganize social-democracy.

Naturally, formulations as the one given by Coriat, defending the introduction of Toyotism in Europe, are searching for a way out of capitalism's crisis, visualizing *within* the latter a new form of work organization, a new form of regulation and a new social order coming from the pact between capital, labour and the state. This conception is based, therefore, on the coexistence and collaboration between social classes, a relation conceived as one of cooperation. It presumes, evidently, the incorporation and acceptance, on the workers side, of the competitive policies formulated by capital. What is the 'Toyota spirit', the 'Toyota Family', 'Nissan, the factory of a new epoch', the 'enterprise union', if not the most pristine expression of this world of work that must live capital's dream?

The most evident consequence of this is the complete distancing of any alternative *beyond capital*, insofar as it adopts and postulates a perspective based on the market, on productivity, on the companies' perspectives. It does not seriously take into account other grave and urgent matters as, for instance, *structural unemployment*, which spreads nowadays worldwide, in impressive magnitudes, and does not spare even Japan, which never had an excess of labour power. This unemployment is the result of these transformations in the production process, of which the Japanese model, *Toyotism*, is the one that has caused the greatest impact on the globalized order of capital. Therefore, we have no doubt in stressing that the *westernization* of Toyotism (disposed of the *singular* features of the history, culture and traditions that characterize the Japanese *Orient*) would in reality conform a decisive achievement of capital *against* labour.

As we indicated previously, we think that it is important to highlight that the 'replacement' of Fordism by Toyotism should not be understood as a *new model of social organization* – which seems obvious to us –, released from the problems of the commodity-producing system. What is less evident and more polemical – but also seems clear to us – is that Toyotism should not even be understood as progress in relation to the capitalism of the Fordist and Taylorist period. In this universe, the question that seems more relevant is the one that asks whether and in what manner the capitalist production realized by the Toyotist model essentially differentiates itself from the *various existing forms* of Fordism. We would like to emphasize here simply that the decreasing distance between *elaboration* and *execution*, between *conception* and *production*, constantly attributed to Toyotism, *is only possible because it realizes itself in the strict and rigorously conceived universe of the commodity-producing system, in the process of capital creation and valorisation.*

In this sense, although we recognize some singularities of the *alienation* of labour in the Toyotist model – reduction of hierarchies, reduction of the factory despotism, a greater 'participation' of workers in the *conception* of the production process – it is important to emphasize that these *singularities* do not suppress the *alienation* of the Toyotist period. The *non-identity* between *individual* and *species-being*, highlighted by Marx in *The Paris Manuscripts*, still exists and is even intensified in several parts of the Japanese working class – and we are not mentioning here the harmful consequences of *toyotization* in its open process of expansion among workers in several countries. The subsumption of the workers' ideals by the ones put forward by capital, the subjection of the *labouring being* to Toyota's 'spirit', to Toyota's 'family', is much more intense; it is *qualitatively* distinct from the one that exists in Fordism. The latter was moved centrally by a more *despotic* logic, while Toyotism is more *consensual*, more *engaging*, more *participative*, in truth, more *manipulative*.

Gramsci made such meaningful indications about the *integral* conception of Fordism, about "the new type of man", in accord with the "new type of work and productive process"; Toyotism surely intensified this *integrality*.[44] Its characteristic form of *alienation* is marked by 'co-opted engagement', which enables capital to appropriate labour's *knowledge* and *actions*. Workers, in the Toyotist integrative logic, must *think* and *act* in relation to capital, to productivity, under the *appearance* of an effective elimination of the divide between *elaboration* and *execution* in the labour process. We say appearance because the effective conception of products, the decision of *what* and *how* to produce does not belong to workers. The result of the labour process, embodied in the product, remains *alien* and *estranged* from the producer, preserving, in all its aspects, the commodity *fetishism*. The existence of a *self-determined activity*, in *all* stages of the production process is an absolute impossibility under Toyotism, since its control remains moved by the logic of the commodity-producing system. *That is why we think that it is possible to say that, in the universe of companies in the period of Japanese production, we witnessed the alienation process of the labouring social being, whose trend gets closer to its limit*. With this precise meaning, it is a *post-fordist alienation*.

These transformations – existing on a larger or smaller scale, depending on several economic, social, political, cultural, etc. conditions, in different countries – had a direct impact on traditional industrial workers, resulting in a metamorphosis of labour's *being*. As it manifested itself, the crisis also intensively

---

44 Antonio Gramsci, "Americanism and Fordism", in *The Gramsci Reader*, ed. David Forgarcs (New York: NYU Press, 2000), 279.

struck the universe of consciousness, of labour's subjectivity, and its representative forms. Unions were stunned and their practices were rarely this defensive. They separated themselves from the 1960s and 1970s *classist social movements and trade unionism* – which demanded *social control* of production – and joined the acritical, negotiator, and *participatory trade unionism*, that generally accepted capital and market orders, questioning only the phenomenic aspect of this order. They abandoned perspectives linked to more global actions that envisioned the emancipation of work, the struggle for socialism and the emancipation of humankind, accepting instead uncritically social-democratization as a goal; and even more perverse, they now debate within the universe of the neoliberal agenda and its ideals. The very defensive position of unions facing the contemporary privatization wave is an expression of what we are pointing out here.

The fall of Eastern Europe, of (neo)Stalinism and of the traditional left – what the predominant ideology called the 'end of socialism' – also had a strong repercussion in worker's organizations and representation, pulling them towards an even more defensive position. So far, the left has been unable to show to broad social contingents that the fall of Eastern Europe has not meant the end of socialism, but the exhaustion of an attempt (thoroughly defeated) to build a society which was not able to go *beyond capital* (to use István Mészáros' expression[45]) – and, therefore, could not constitute itself even as a *socialist society*.

Unions deeply trailed the institutionalization path and increasingly distanced themselves from independent class movements. They separated themselves from the actions of *classist trade unionism and anticapitalistic social movements* – whose aim was the social control of production and were so intense in previous decades – subjecting themselves to participate inside the order. They devised their movements according to values coming from the sociability of market and capital. The world of work did not find, in its predominant trends, especially in its union representation, a disposition to anticapitalistic struggles. The various forms of class resistance found barriers in the lack of representatives with a consciousness pointing *beyond capital*. Again, this was a deeply problematic decade, with the most acute crisis experienced by the world of work, in this 'lost century'. A century that started with a revolution which, in its origins, in 1917, seemed capable of initiating the cycle of

---

45   István Mészáros, "Il Rinnovamento del Marxismo e l'Attualità Storica dell'Ofensiva Socialista", *Problemi del Socialismo*, no. 23 (1982); "Marxism Today: an Interview with István Mészáros", interview by Chris Arthur and Joseph McCarney, *Monthly Review*, vol. 39/3 (1993).

deconstruction of capitalism, and it is about to end in the darkest manner to those who are critics of capital.

This context, in which the most serious problems were only mentioned here, critically affected (and still affects) the world of work, particularly industrial workers. What were the most evident consequences that deserve a deeper analysis? Is the working class disappearing[46]? Does the retraction of the industrial workers, in high income countries, inevitably result in the loss of reference and relevance of the *class-that-lives-from-labour*? Does the category *labour*, in this stage of capitalism, no longer have a centrality to understand human activity, human *praxis*[47]? Should the so-called crisis of the 'labour society' be understood as the end of the *labour revolution*[48]? Is labour no longer the *proto-form* of *the* social being's activities – reminding us of Lukács – or the eternal and natural necessity to realize the metabolism between humans and nature – reminding us of Marx[49]? The questions are acute and the answers are also very complex.

The goal of this book, in the next chapter, is to attempt to indicate some *preliminary* elements that exist nowadays in the world of work and that have a direct impact on workers' *movement*, on their class consciousness, and on their *subjectivity*.

---

46   André Gorz, *Farewell to the Working Class: an Essay on Post-Industrial Socialism* (London: Pluto Press, 1982); "The New Agenda", *New Left Review*, no. 184 (1990).

47   Claus Offe, "Trabalho como Categoria Sociológica Fundamental?", *Trabalho & Sociedade*, vol. 1 (1989); Jürgen Habermas, "The New Obscurity", in *The New Conservatism: Cultural Criticism and the Historians' Debate* (Cambridge: Polity Press, 1989).

48   Kurz, *O Colapso da Modernização*.

49   György Lukács, *Ontologia dell'Essere Sociale I and II* (Roma: Riuniti, 1976, 1981); Karl Marx, "Capital. Volume 1: The Process of Production of Capital", in *Karl Marx & Friedrich Engels, Collected Works, vol. 35* (London: Lawrence & Wishart, 1996), 187–188.

CHAPTER 2

Metamorphoses in the World of Work

In contemporary capitalism, we observe multiple processes in the world of work: on one hand, there was a *de-proletarianization of industrial labour* in capitalist advanced countries, with a greater or lesser impact in industrialized areas of the Global South. In other words, there was a decrease in the number of traditional industrial workers. However, in parallel, there was an expressive expansion of wage-labour, as a result of its vast extension in the service sector; it can be observed as a meaningful process in which work became more heterogeneous, expressed also in the increasing integration of women into labour markets. We also witness an intensified *sub-proletarianization*, in the expansion of part-time, temporary, subcontracted and 'outsourced' labour, which marks the *dual society* of advanced capitalism. *Gastarbeiters*, in Germany, and *Lavoro nero*, in Italy, are examples of this enormous contingent of immigrant labour, which are going to the so-called First World, searching for what remains of the *welfare state* – reversing the migration flows of previous decades from core countries to periphery countries.

The most brutal result of these transformations is the expansion, without any precedent in modern times, of a worldwide *structural unemployment*. It is possible to say, synthetically, that there is a contradictory process in which, on one side, there is a decreasing number of industrial workers; and, on the other, there is an increase in the ranks of the subproletariat, of precarious work and of wage-labour in the service sector. This also integrates women's labour and excludes the young and the old. There is, therefore, a process where the working class becomes more *heterogeneous, fragmented and complex*.

We will try, in the following pages, to give examples of the current multiple and contradictory process in the world of work. We will do this providing some data, only with the aim of illustrating these trends.

We start with the question of de-proletarianization of industrial work. In France, in 1962, industrial workers were 7.488 million. In 1975, this number reaches 8.118 million and, in 1989, decreases to 7.121 million. While in 1962 it represented 39% of the working population, in 1989 diminished to 29.6%.[1]

---

1 Data extracted from *Economie et Statistiques*, L'INSEE, quoted by Alain Bihr, "Le Prolétariat Dans Tous Ses Éclats", *Le Monde Diplomatique*, n. 444 (1991). See also Alain Bihr, *Du 'Grand Soir' a 'l' Alternative': le Mouvement Ouvrier Européen en Crise* (Paris: Les Éditions Ouvrières, 1991), 87–108.

Frank Annunziato, referring to the oscillations in labour power in United States, provides the following numbers (in the thousands):

TABLE 1   Oscillations in labour power in United States (1980–1986)

Sector	1980	1986	Percent change
Agriculture	3,426	2,917	− 14.8%
Mining	1,027	724	− 29.5%
Construction	4,346	4.906	+ 12.8%
Manufacture	20,286	18,994	− 6.3%
Transport and civil service	5,146	5,719	+ 11.1%
Large commerce	5,275	5,735	+ 8.7%
Small commerce	15,035	17,845	+ 18.6%
Finance, insurance and real state	5,159	6,297	+ 22.0%
Government	16,241	16,711	+ 2.8%
Services	11,390	22,531	+ 97.8%

SOURCE: STATISTICAL ABSTRACT OF THE UNITED STATES, 1988, PUBLISHED BY UNITED STATES DEPARTMENT OF COMMERCE, REPRODUCED IN FRANK ANNUNZIATO, "IL FORDISMO NELLA CRITICA DI GRAMSCI E NELLA REALTÀ STATUNITENSE CONTEMPORANEA." CRITICA MARXISTA, NO. 6 (1989), 107

This data shows, on one side, the reduction of workers in industry (and also in mining and agriculture); on the other, an explosive growth in the service sector, which according to the author includes the 'service industry', large and small commerce, finance, insurance, real state, hotel businesses, restaurants, personal services, business services, entertainment, health, legal services and general services.[2]

The reduction of industrial workers also took place in Italy, where a little more than a million jobs were eliminated. The share of workers in industry decreased from 40%, in 1980, to around 30%, in 1990.[3]

---

2 Frank Annunziato, "Il Fordismo nella Critica di Gramsci e nella Realtà Statunitense Contemporanea", *Critica Marxista*, no. 6 (1989), 107.
3 Andrea Stuppini, "Chi Sono e che Cosa Vogliono i Nuovi Operai", *Mondo Operaio*, no. 2, Anno 44 (1991), 50.

Another author, in a prospective essay – not particularly concerned with an empirical demonstration – tries to indicate some of the ongoing trends, resulting from the technological revolution. He reminds us that projections made by the Japanese businesses community aim to "completely eliminate manual jobs in the Japanese industry by the end of the century. Although there is a certain nationalism in this, the projection of this goal should be taken seriously".[4]

About Canada, the author reproduces information in a report from the *Science Council of Canada* (n. 33, 1982), which "predicts that 25% of workers will lose their jobs until the end of the century, as a consequence of automation".[5]

It is possible to say that in most industrialized countries of Western Europe, the proportion of workers in industry represented around 40% of the working population in the beginning of the 1940s. Nowadays, this proportion is around 30%. Projections are that it will decrease to 20% or 25% at the beginning of the next century.[6]

This data and trends show a clear reduction of industrial workers, especially in advanced capitalist countries, as a result either of the recession context or of automation, robotics and microelectronics, creating a massive rate of structural unemployment.

Alongside this trend, there is another extremely significant element, resulting from the *sub-proletarianization* of work, in the forms of precarious work, part-time, temporary, subcontracted, 'outsourced', linked to the 'informal economy', etc. As Alain Bihr says, these various categories of workers have in common the precariousness of both jobs and incomes; the deregulation of existent laws or agreements on working conditions; the regression of social, economic and cultural rights; and the lack of union protection and expression; all of this resulting in an extreme individualization of wage relations.[7]

As an example, between 1982 and 1988 in France, while there was a reduction in 501,000 full-time jobs, there was an increase in 111,000 *part-time* ones.[8] In another study, Bihr adds that this 'atypical' form of work did not stop developing after the crisis; between 1982 and 1986, the number of part-time workers increased by 21.35%.[9] In 1988, another author says 23.2% of wageworkers from

---

4 Adam Schaff, *A Sociedade Informática* (São Paulo: Brasiliense/Unesp, 1990), 28.
5 Ibid.
6 André Gorz, "Pourquoi la Societé Salariale a Besoin de Nouveux Valets", *Le Monde Diplomatique*, no. 22 (1990); "O Futuro da Classe Operária", *Revista Internacional, Revista Internacional, Quinzena*, no. 101 (1990).
7 Bihr, *Du 'Grand Soir'*, 89.
8 Bihr, "Le Prolétariat".
9 Bihr, *Du 'Grand Soir'*, 88–89.

the European Economic Community were part-time or temporary workers.[10] This data goes in the same direction of Harvey's:

> the current trend in labour markets is to reduce the number of 'core' workers and to rely increasingly upon a work force that can quickly be taken on board and equally quickly and costlessly be laid off when times get bad. In Britain, 'flexible workers' increased by 16 percent resulting in 8.1 million flexible workers between 1981 and 1985, while permanent jobs decreased by 6 percent to 15.6 million [...] Over roughly the same time period, nearly one third of the ten million new jobs created in the USA were thought to be in the temporary category.[11]

André Gorz adds that approximately 35% to 50% of the working population in Great Britain, France, Germany and United States is unemployed or doing precarious, part-time work – the 'post-industrial proletariat', as Gorz named them – exposing the real dimension of what some called the 'dual society'.[12]

In other words, while several advanced capitalist countries witnessed a decrease in full-time jobs, they have watched, in parallel, an increase in the forms of sub-proletarianization, through the expansion of part-time, precarious, temporary, subcontracted, etc. workers. According to Helena Hirata, 20% of women in Japan, in 1980, were working in part-time, precarious conditions: "official statistics, in 1980, counted 2,560 million women working at part-time jobs, three years later the *Economisto* periodical, from Tokyo, estimated 5 million women working in part-time jobs".[13]

Women are a large share of this increase in the workforce and this is another *important feature* of the ongoing transformations inside the working class. The latter is not 'exclusively' male, but has a massive contingent of women, not only in industries like textiles, in which they were always substantial, but in new segments like microelectronics, not to mention the services sector. This change in the productive structure and in labour market enabled the integration and an increased exploitation of women's workforce in part-time jobs and 'household' work subordinated to capital (as the one made for Benetton). This

---

10   Stuppini, "Chi Sono".
11   David Harvey, *The Condition of Postmodernity: An Enquiry into the Origins of Cultural Change* (Oxford: Blackwell Publishers, 1990), 152.
12   André Gorz, "The New Agenda", *New Left Review*, no. 184 (1990), 42; "Pourquoi la Societé Salariale".
13   Helena Hirata, "Trabalho, Família e Relações Homem/Mulher: Reflexões a Partir do Caso Japonês", *Revista Brasileira de Ciências* Sociais, vol. 1, no. 2 (1986), 9.

happened in such a way that, in Italy, approximately a million jobs created in the 1980s employed women, mostly in the service sector – but with repercussions also in factories.[14] Of the total part-time jobs created in France, between 1982 and 1986, more than 80% were filled by the female workforce.[15] It is possible to say that this number has been increasing in practically every country and, despite national differences, women represent more than 40% of the workforce in many advanced capitalist countries.[16]

Female presence in the world of work allows us to add that if class consciousness is a complex articulation – comprising identity and heterogeneity – between *singularities* living *materially* and *subjectively* a particular situation in the production process and in social life, both the contradictions between *individuals* and their *class* and the one between *class* and *gender* became sharper nowadays. The *class-that-lives-from-labour* is male and female. It is, therefore, diverse, heterogeneous and complex. In this sense, a critique of capital, as a social relation, must apprehend the exploitation dimension of capital/labour relations and also the oppression of man/woman relations, in the sense that the struggle to constitute the *species-being-for-itself* enables also the emancipation of women.[17]

Besides the de-proletarianization of industrial work, the integration of female labour and the sub-proletarianization of work through part-time and temporary jobs, there is another feature in this diverse context: an intensive process of transformation of medium segments into wage labour, resulting from the expansion of the services sector. We saw that, in the case of United States, the service sector – in the broad sense defined by the Department of

---

14   Stuppini, "Chi Sono", 50.
15   Bihr, *Du 'Grand Soir'*, 89.
16   Harvey, *The Condition of Postmodernity*, 155; Richard Freeman, "Pueden Sobrevivir los Sindicatos en la Sociedad Pos-industrial", *Simpósio Internacional sobre las Perspectivas Futuras del Sindicalismo*. Confédération des Syndicats Chrétiens, Brussels (1986).
17   "In a de-alienated world, not dominated by the tendency to appropriate, individuals will no longer be constituted as particular beings. Individual personality, nowadays an exception, will be typical in society. Moral norms will not be imposed from outside to a person enclosed in her particularism. Individuals will be capable of [...] humanizing their impulses, instead of repressing them [...] will be capable of humanizing their emotions [...]. When facing social conflicts we choose between alternatives, and simultaneously opt for a determined future of relations between sexes. We elect relations between free and equal individuals, relations that, in all aspects of human life, are realized without any tendency to appropriate and are characterized by its richness, profundity and sincerity". Agnes Heller, "El futuro de las relaciones entre los sexos", in *La Revolución de la Vida Cotidiana*. (Barcelona: Ed. Península, 1982), 65–66. See also Hirata, "Trabalho, Família e Relações Homem/Mulher".

Commerce's census – grew to 97.8% between 1980 and 1986, corresponding to more than 60% of all the jobs (not including the government).[18]

In Italy, "nowadays occupation in tertiary and service sector grows, [it] currently is above 60% of total jobs".[19] It is known that this tendency exists in almost all core countries.

It is possible to point out that

> in these researches about the structure and tendencies of development in highly industrialized western societies, increasingly often, we find their characterization as a 'services society'. This refers to the absolute and relative growth of the 'tertiary sector', that is, the 'service sector'.[20]

It must be stressed, however, that acknowledging this expansion does not lead to accept the thesis of *post-industrial* or *post-capitalist* societies, since it is preserved,

> at least indirectly, the unproductive character, in the sense of capitalist global production, of most services. They are not autonomous sectors of capital accumulation; on the contrary, the services sector remains dependent on industrial accumulation and, therefore, on the capacity of these industries to realize surplus value in the world market. Only when this capacity is maintained in the national economy, as a whole, can industrial and non-industrial (related to people) services survive and expand.[21]

Finally, there is another very important consequence, inside the working class, that has a two-sided direction: in parallel to the *quantitative* reduction of traditional industrial workers, there is also a *qualitative* change in work's *form of being* that impels, on one side, towards greater *skills* in work, and, on the other side, towards greater *deskilling*.

We can start with the first element. The reduction in the *variable* dimension of capital, due to the increase of its *constant* part – or, in other words, the replacement of *living labour* for *dead labour* – offers, as a tendency, in the

---

18   Annunziato, "Il Fordismo nella Critica di Gramsci", 107.
19   Stuppini, "Chi Sono", 50.
20   Claus Offe & Johannes Berger, "A Dinâmica do Desenvolvimento do Setor de Serviços", *Trabalho & Sociedade*, vol. 2 (1991), 11.
21   Robert Kurz, *O Colapso da Modernização: Da Derrocada do Socialismo de Caserna à Crise da Economia Mundial* (São Paulo: Paz e Terra, 1992), 209.

most advanced production units, the possibility of approximating the worker to what Marx called the "overseer and regulator" of the production process.[22] However, the complete realization of this tendency is rendered impossible by capital's logic itself. This long quote from Marx, in which he mentions the characterization we used above, is illuminating:

> the exchange of living labour for objectified [...] is the ultimate development of the *value relationship* and of production based on value. Its presupposition is and remains the sheer volume of immediate labour time, the quantity of labour employed, as the decisive factor in the production of wealth. But in the degree in which large-scale industry develops, the creation of real wealth becomes less dependent upon labour time and the quantity of labour employed than upon the power of the agents set in motion during labour time. And their power – their *powerful effectiveness* – in turn bears no relation to the immediate labour time which their production costs, but depends, rather, upon the general level of development of science and the progress of technology, or on the application of science to production [...] Real wealth manifests itself rather – and this is revealed by large-scale industry – in the immense disproportion between the labour time employed and its product, and similarly in the qualitative disproportion between labour reduced to a pure abstraction and the power of the production process which it oversees. Labour no longer appears so much as included in the production process, but rather man relates himself to that process as its overseer and regulator [...] No longer does the worker interpose a modified natural object as an intermediate element between the object and himself; now he interposes the natural process, which he transforms into an industrial one, as an intermediary between himself and inorganic nature, which he makes himself master of. He stands beside the production process, rather than being its main agent. Once this transformation has taken place, it is neither the immediate labour performed by man himself, nor the time for which he works, but the appropriation of his own general productive power, his comprehension of Nature and domination of it by virtue of his being a social entity – in a word, the development of the social individual – that appears as the cornerstone of production and wealth. The *theft of alien labour time, which is the basis of present wealth,* appears to be a miserable

---

22   Karl Marx, "Outlines of the Critique of Political Economy" in *Karl Marx & Friedrich Engels, Collected Works, vol. 29* (London: Lawrence & Wishart, 1987), 91.

> foundation compared to this newly developed one, the foundation created by large-scale industry itself. As soon as labour in its immediate form has ceased to be the great source of wealth, labour time ceases and must cease to be its measure, and therefore exchange value [must cease to be the measure] of use value. The *surplus labour of the masses* has ceased to be the condition for the development of general wealth, just as the *non-labour of a few* has ceased to be the condition for the development of the general powers of the human mind. As a result, production based upon exchange value collapses [...] Free development of individualities, and hence not the reduction of necessary labour time in order to posit surplus labour, but in general the reduction of the necessary labour of society to a minimum, to which then corresponds the artistic, scientific, etc., development of individuals, made possible by the time thus set free and the means produced for all of them.[23]

It becomes evident, however, that this abstraction is impossible in capitalist societies. As Marx himself explains, following the excerpt above:

> by striving to reduce labour time to a minimum, while, on the other hand, positing labour time as the sole measure and source of wealth, capital itself is a contradiction-in-process. It therefore diminishes labour time in the form of necessary labour time in order to increase it in the form of superfluous labour time; it thus posits superfluous labour time to an increasing degree as a condition – *question de vie et de mort* – for necessary labour time. On the one hand, therefore, it calls into life all the powers of science and Nature, and of social combination and social intercourse, in order to make the creation of wealth (relatively) independent of the labour time employed for that purpose. On the other hand, it wishes the enormous social forces thus created to be measured by labour time and to confine them within the limits necessary to maintain as value the value already created. The productive forces and social relations – two different aspects of the development of the social individual – appear to capital merely as the means, and *are* merely the means, for it to carry on production on its restricted basis. In fact, however, they are the material conditions for exploding that basis.[24]

---

23 Marx, "Outlines of the Critique", 90–91.
24 Ibid., 91–92.

Therefore, the tendency indicated by Marx – which to be completely fulfilled presupposes a rupture with capital's logic – shows that as long as the capitalist mode of production endures, labour as the source that creates value cannot be eliminated. What can occur are changes inside the labour process – as a result of scientific and technological developments – that are based more on the *skilled* dimension of labour, more on the *intellectualization of social labour*. This is illuminated in the following passage:

> with the development of the *real subsumption of labour under capital* or the *specifically capitalist mode of production* it is not the individual worker but rather a *socially combined labour capacity* that is more and more the *real executor* of the labour process as a whole, and since the different labour capacities which cooperate together to form the productive machine as a whole contribute in very different ways to the direct process by which the commodity, or, more appropriate here, the product, is formed, one working more with his hands, another more with his brain, one as a *manager, engineer* – or technician, etc., another as an *overlooker*, the third directly as a manual worker, or even a mere assistant, more and more of the *functions of labour capacity* are included under the direct concept of *productive labour*, and their repositories under the concept of *productive workers*, workers directly exploited by capital and altogether *subordinated* to its valorisation and production process. If one considers the *total worker* constituting the workshop, his *combined activity* is directly realised *materialiter* in a *total product* which is at the same time a *total quantity of commodities*, and in this connection, it is a matter of complete indifference whether the function of the individual worker, who is only a constituent element of this total worker, stands close to direct manual labour or is far away from it.[25]

The case of the automated Japanese factory Fujitsu Fanuc – an example of technological development – is illuminating. More than 400 robots make other robots, for 24 hours per day. Almost 400 people work mornings and afternoons. With traditional methods, it would take 4,000 workers to reach the same level of production. On average, each month, eight robots are broken and the workers' task is basically to prevent damage or replace broken robots, which means discontinuous and unpredictable work. There are 1,700 people working in the

---

25　Karl Marx, "Chapter Six. Results of the Direct Production Process", in *Karl Marx & Friedrich Engels, Collected Works, vol. 34* (London: Lawrence & Wishart, 1994), 443–444.

company's research, management and commerce sectors.²⁶ Although this is an example of one country and of *singular* factories, it is possible to note, on one side, that not even their labour was eliminated, but there was an *intellectualization* of parts of the working class . In this atypical example, however, workers do not directly transform material objects, but oversee the production process in computerized machines, programming them and fixing robots if needed.²⁷

To assume the generalization of this tendency under contemporary capitalism, including the huge number of workers in the Global South, would be a great misunderstanding. Were this the case, the result would inevitably be the destruction of the market economy itself, due to the impossibility of carrying out capital accumulation. Neither consumers nor wageworkers, only robots would participate in the market. Therefore, the simple survival of capitalist economy would be compromised.²⁸

Reflecting also on a *trend* towards a greater skilling and intellectualization of labour, another author develops the thesis that the image of manual worker cannot be used to comprehend the new industrial workers. The latter has changed in several more qualified sectors, exemplified by overseer operators, maintenance technicians, programmers, quality controllers, research technicians, engineers responsible for technical coordination and production management. Old divisions would be challenged by the necessary cooperation among workers.²⁹

There are, therefore, mutations in the universe of the working class, that differ in each industry, each sector, etc. Deskilling occurred in several industries; the labour power diminished in others, such as mining, metallurgy and shipbuilding. It almost disappeared in sectors that were fully computerised, such as the graphic industry; and it reskilled in others where one can observe

> the formation of a particular segment of 'workers-technicians' endowed with high responsibilities, holding professional features and cultural references perceptibly distinct from other workers. They can be founded, for instance, in coordinating positions in operational booths of blast furnaces, melt shops, [and] continuous casting [...] There is a similar phenomenon in the car industry with the creation of 'technicians-coordinators' in

---

26   Gorz, "O Futuro da Classe Operária", 28.
27   Ibid.
28   Ernst Mandel, "Marx, la Crise Actuelle et l'Avenir du Travail Humain", *Quatrième Internationale*, no. 20 (1986), 16–17.
29   Jean Lojkine, *A Classe Operária em Mutações* (São Paulo: Oficina de Livros, 1990), 30–31.

charge of repair and maintenance of highly automated plants, helped by professionals at lower positions and with different skills.[30]

Alongside this tendency, another can be added related to the *deskilling* of several industrial sectors, impacted by a set of transformations which resulted, on one side, in *de-specialization* of the industrial worker coming from Fordism and, on the other side, in a mass of workers that oscillates between temporary (without any job guarantee), partial (precariously integrated into companies),[31] subcontracted, outsourced (which occurs also in very skilled sectors) and workers in the 'informal economy'. All in all, this resulted in this large number that accounts for 50% of the working population in advanced capitalist countries – including also the unemployed – which some authors call the *post-industrial proletariat,* but we prefer to denominate it the *modern subproletariat.*

Regarding the *de-specialization* of professional industrial workers, resulting from the creation of 'multifunctional workers' introduced by Toyotism, it is relevant to remember that this process also meant an attack on the professional knowledge of skilled workers, reducing their power over production and increasing labour intensity. Skilled workers organized strikes against *de-specialization*, viewing it as an attack upon their professions and qualifications, as well as upon the power to negotiate which their skills endowed to them.[32] We already mentioned, previously, the limited character of *polyvalence* introduced by the Japanese model.

The segmentation of the working class intensified in such a way that is possible to indicate that at the *core* of the production process a group of workers can be found, diminishing worldwide, which remains in full time jobs in factories, with greater stability and more integrated to the companies. With some advantages resulting from this 'greater integration', this segment is more adaptable, flexible and has greater geographical mobility. As David Harvey says:

---

30   Ibid., 32.
31   See Bihr, *Du 'Grand Soir'*, 88–89.
32   Benjamin Coriat, *Pensar al Revés: Trabajo y Organización en la Empresa Japonesa* (Ciudad de México: Siglo XXI, 1992), 41. See also, Michel Freyssenet, "A Divisão Capitalista do Trabalho", *Tempo Social*, vol. 1, no. 2 (1989), who says that with the development of automation "[...] a movement is reproduced [...] that is, the deskilling of certain 'super-skilled' tasks that emerged in the previous moment of the deskilling-superskilling of labour. Therefore, this concerns mainly the maintenance tasks and the ones that make machine-tools".

potential costs of laying off core employees in time of difficulty may, however, lead a company to sub-contract even high-level functions (varying from design to advertising and financial management), leaving the core group of managers relatively small.[33]

The periphery of the labour power comprises two different subgroups: the first consists of "full-time employees with skills that are readily available in the labour market, such as clerical, secretarial, routine and lesser skilled manual work". This subgroup tends to be characterized by high labour turnover rates. The second group in the labour periphery "provides even greater numerical flexibility and includes part-timers, casuals, fixed term contract staff, temporaries, sub-contractors and public subsidy trainees, with even less job security than the first peripheral group". This segment has significantly grown in recent years (following the classification of the *Institute of Personnel Management*[34]).

Therefore, while there is a tendency to *qualify* labour, there is also the development of an intense process of *deskilling* of workers, which results in a contradictory process of *superskilling* several production sectors and *deskilling* others.[35]

These elements that we presented here enable us to indicate that there is not a generalized and univocal tendency when we reflect on the world of work. There is, in fact, as we tried to show, a contradictory and multiform process. This made the *class-that-lives-from-labour* more complex, fragmented and heterogeneous. Therefore, it is possible to observe, on one side, an effective process of *intellectualization of manual labour,* on the other, in a radically reversed sense, an intensified *deskilling* and even a *sub-proletarianization* in precarious, informal, temporary, part-time and subcontracted, labour. If it is possible to say that the first tendency – the *intellectualization of manual labour* – is, ideally, more coherent and compatible with the enormous technological development, the second – *deskilling* – is also fully in tune with capitalist mode of

---

33 Harvey, *The Condition of Postmodernity*, 150.
34 See Harvey, *The Condition of Postmodernity*, 150–151.
35 See Michel Freyssenet's conclusion: "[...] there is not a generalized movement of deskilling or a movement of general increase in skilling, but a contradictory movement of *deskilling the labours of some and 'superskilling' the labour of others*; that is, there is a polarization of the skills required, which results in a particular form of labour division. The latter is characterized by a change in the social distribution of the 'intelligence' in production. Part of this 'intelligence' is 'incorporated' in the machines and the other part is distributed between a great number of workers by the activities of a restrict number of persons, in charge of the (impossible) task of thinking in advance the totality of the labour process [...]". Freyssenet, "A Divisão Capitalista do Trabalho", 75.

production, with its *destructive logic* and with its *decreasing rate of utilization of goods and services*.[36] We also saw that there was a significant incorporation of women's labour in the world of production, and an expressive expansion of the working class through wage labour in the service sector. All this enables us to conclude that industrial workers will not disappear as fast as imagined and, *fundamentally*, it is not possible to envision, not even in a distant world, any possibility to eliminate the *class-that-lives-from-labour* .

36   István Mészáros, *Beyond Capital: Towards a Theory of Transition* (London: Merlin Press, 1995), 580–600.

CHAPTER 3

Dimensions of the Trade Unionism's Contemporary Crisis
Dilemmas and Challenges

We would like to now discuss the *repercussions that these metamorphoses had on the working-class movements*. We start by raising the following questions: what are the consequences brought by the several and significant changes in the world of work to the universe of subjectivity and the labouring social being's consciousness? Particularly, which results did these transformations have on the workers' *class actions*, on their representative and mediating institutions, like trade unions, which are living, as known, a very critical situation? What are the most acute evidence, dimensions and meanings of the *contemporary union's crisis*? Do they show enough vitality to go beyond defensive actions and to restore the most expressive meaning of trade union's action?[1]

We will start this discussion, that deals with the *contemporary crisis of trade unions*, answering the following questions: 1) What are the essential outlines and dimensions of this crisis? 2) Why could it be said, effectively, that there is a *trade union crisis*? 3) In this situation, what are the main challenges to labour movements?

As analysed in detail in the first part of this book, the current metamorphoses in the world of work affected the working-class' *form of being*, making it more heterogeneous, fragmented and complex. These transformations also intensively impacted trade unions on a world scale. The most evident expression of this crisis is the clearly *decreasing trend of unionisation rates*, especially in the 1980s.

We start discussing this topic presenting, in an ascending order, the levels or rates of unionisation in several capitalist countries:

---

[1] Besides these questions, we could add those related to subordinated countries: with changes in the labour process of several advanced countries, what repercussions and consequences can be observed in countries like Brazil? Which analytical mediations are indispensable when one thinks about the reality of the world of work in the advanced capitalist countries and its parallels and developments in countries like Brazil? The particularity of our working-class points to convergent or divergent paths to those being trailed by the world of work in core countries? Will we follow or not the trends of advanced capitalism? These questions lead us to the Brazilian case. We tried to answer them, in a certain sense, in the essay *O Novo Sindicalismo* (São Paulo: Scritta, 1991).

TABLE 2   Unionization Rates, 1988*

Unionization rate:	1988
France:	12%
Spain:	16%
United States:	16.8%
Turkey:	18.8%
Greece:	25%
Low Countries:	25%
Switzerland:	26%
Japan:	26.8%
Portugal:	30%
Germany:	33.8%
Canada:	34.6%
Italy:	39.6%
United Kingdom:	41.5%
Australia:	42%
Austria:	45.7%
Luxemburg:	49.7%
New Zealand:	50.5%
Ireland:	52.4%
Belgium:	53%
Norway:	55.1%
Finland:	71%
Denmark:	73.2%
Netherlands:	78.3%
Sweden:	85.3%

* Rates for Netherlands, 1989; Ireland, 1987; Luxemburg, 1989; New Zealand, 1990; Spain, 1985; Switzerland, 1987; Turkey, 1987. Rates for Portugal and Greece are estimations

SOURCE: ÉVOLUTION DU TAUX DE SYNDICALISATION, IN *RAPPORT ANNUEL*, OCDE, 1992, CHAPTER 4, ELABORATED BY JELLE VISSER AND REVIEWED BY OECD SECRETARIAT

J. Visser's study about de-unionisation gives detailed information supporting recent trends of unionisation rates. He says that between 1980–1990, in most western industrialized capitalist countries, the unionisation rate – that is, the relation between unionised workers and the wage population – has decreased. In Western Europe as a whole – excluding Spain, Portugal and Greece – this rate has been reduced from 41%, in 1980, to 34%, in 1989. If the three countries mentioned above were counted, the rate would be further reduced. One can remember, for comparative purposes, that Japan's unionisation fell from 30% to 25% in the same period, and the United States' rate was reduced from 23% to 16%.[2] In Spain, France, Great Britain, Low Countries and, to a lesser extent, Italy, Ireland, Greece and Portugal, there was a strong reduction in unionisation rates and a decline in the total number of members (as happened in Spain, France and Great Britain). There was a slight reduction, especially in the second half of the decade, in Belgium, Luxemburg, West Germany, Austria and Denmark. In Finland, Norway and Sweden trade unions increased their members during the 1980s, but there was a change in this trend in 1988.[3] Visser also claims that there is nothing similar to this decrease in the intensity of unionisation rates at any other point in post-war trade unions' history.[4]

Nevertheless, this de-unionisation trend should not be confused with a uniformization of trade unions. In Sweden, for instance, more than 80% of wageworkers are unionised. Alongside Belgium and Austria, it constitutes the group of countries with higher rates of unionisation. Italy, Great Britain and Germany form an intermediate group, while France, Spain and the US are further down, followed by Japan, the Low Countries and Switzerland.[5]

---

2   Jelle Visser, "Syndicalisme et Désyndicalisation", *Le Mouvement Social*, no. 162 (1993).
3   Ibid., 19.
4   Ibid.
5   Ibid., 24. The paper "Syndicalisme et Désyndicalisation", by J. Visser, is in *Le Mouvement Social*, no. 162 (january-march 1993). The volume is entitled *Syndicats D'Europe* (organized by Jacques Freyssinet) and brings a detailed analysis of unions' crisis in advanced capitalist countries, addressing several aspects, such as: the changes inside trade unions movements; the expansion of female workforce; the emergence of new sectors, like service; the national particularities that make it difficult to generalize the diversity of cases; union's loss of power; their choices to act as a social movements or as institutionalized organizations; and the analysis of the several hypothesis explaining de-unionisation. It is important to remind that, according to Visser (27–28), *unionisation rates are a starting point in the study of trade unionism, but they cannot be taken as indispensable elements when the question is to apprehend the real meaning of union activism, marked by many differences between realities apparently similar*. About the unions' crisis, see also the special issue published in *El País*, in 24 January, 1993, p. 1–8, which brings a good overview of the crisis of trade unions in Europe. See also, Richard Freeman, "Pueden Sobrivivir los Sindicatos en la Sociedad Pos-industrial", *Simpósio Internacional Sobre las Perspectivas Futuras del Sindicalismo*. Confédération des Syndicats Chrétiens (1986), especially about the ongoing trends in North American trade unions; John Kelly, *Labour and the Unions* (London: Verso, 1987), about the tendencies in English trade unionism; and Leôncio M. Rodrigues "A Crise do Sindicalismo no Primeiro Mundo", *Folha de São Paulo*, 22 March, 1993, and "A Sindicalização da Classe Média", *Folha de São Paulo*, 24 May, 1993.

Another decisive element in the development and expansion of the trade unions' crisis can be found in the abyss between workers with 'stability', on one side, and the precarious ones, at the other. The deepening of this social chasm inside the working class severely undermines trade union's power, historically linked to workers with 'stability' and, so far, incapable of integrating part-time, temporary, precarious, informal, etc. workers. Therefore, *the vertical trade unionism begins to fall apart, a legacy of Fordism that is corporatist and more linked to professional sectors*. It has been incapable of acting as a more *horizontal trade unionism*, endowed with a greater inclusiveness that privileges relations between sectors and professions, capable of bringing together different groups of workers, from the ones with greater 'stability' to the ones in precarious jobs, in the informal economy, etc.[6]

The fragmented, more heterogeneous and complex character of the *class-that-lives-from-labour*, questions traditional trade unionism at its *roots* and also makes the unionisation of other segments of the working class more difficult. As Visser says, trade unions had been facing difficulties in integrating women, commerce and office workers, people employed by small businesses and part-time workers. With the exception of some countries such as Sweden, Denmark and Finland, women have lower unionisation rates. Non-manual labour workers are still behind manual ones, even if the difference between them is lower than it was in the past, especially in Scandinavia. Industrial workers still join unions in greater numbers than workers in commerce, hospitality and private finances.[7] Part-time, immigrant, temporary, women, young and small business workers seem to be part of these diverse relations that make it more difficult to increase unionisation rates. Women's participation in labour market, for instance, is higher as part-time, temporary, etc. Perhaps this *helps* to understand the lower female unionisation rates. Regarding the low rates of unionisation among younger workers, Visser says that it is difficult to claim if it is a temporary phenomenon or the prelude to a new tendency.[8]

Alongside these processes that push to de-unionisation, there were important developments in organizing intermediate sectors of wageworkers. In England, where trade unions have recurred to mergers as a way to resist the neoliberal landslide, there was recently a significant case of organic fusion among several public sector trade unions, which created the countries'

---

6 Alain Bihr, *Du 'Grand Soir' a 'l' Alternative': le Mouvement Ouvrier Européen en Crise* (Paris: Les Éditions Ouvrières, 1991), 106.
7 Visser, "Syndicalisme et Désyndicalisation.", 21–22.
8 Ibid., 23.

strongest one – called *Unison* – that has about 1,400,000 members.[9] It is known that between 1979–1985 the number of Trade Union Congress' (TUC) members declined from 12.2 million to 9.5 million – a decrease of 22% – demonstrating the trend we mentioned above. If we take into account the total members, linked or not to TUC, reduction in the same period was 18.5%, from 13.5 million to 11 million.[10] In this context, the development of trade unionism in the intermediary segments of wageworkers is expressive:

> if we consider the private sector alone, in mid-1980s, non-manual workers represented, in Austria, 22% of all union members; in Denmark, 24%; in Germany, 18%; in the Netherlands, 16%; in Norway, 17%; in Sweden, 23%; in Switzerland, 25%. Currently, in Germany, 1 in 3 unionised workers belongs to the 'middle class', while in Norway and the Netherlands estimations say that half of unionised workers are non-manual. In France, where trade unions' crisis is particularly acute, the percentage of non-manual workers within all unionised workers (in private and public sectors) is above 50%. In Norway, is 48%; in Great Britain, 40%; in Sweden, 36%; in Austria, 35%; in Denmark, 32%; in Italy, 20%.[11]

However, as Leôncio Martins Rodrigues stresses, this expansion of trade unionism among employees in public and private sectors was not enough, in most countries, to make up for the decline of manual workers' unionisation rates.[12]

Another consequence of these changes is the intensification of neo-corporatist tendencies that tries to preserve the interests of workers with stability, linked to unions, against precarious, outsourced, part-time, etc. segments of the working class – which we called *subproletariat*. This is not a state corporatism, closer to countries like Brazil, Mexico and Argentina, but a social corporatism, almost exclusively associated with professional spheres. It is increasingly *exclusionary and partial* – features intensified by worker's fragmentation – instead of opening to seek new organizational forms capable of articulating broad and different sectors of the contemporary working class. As Alain Bihr stresses, there is a rising risk that this type of corporatism expands.[13]

These transformations also impacted strikes, diminishing in a certain way their efficiency, as a result of the fragmentation and the more heterogeneous character

---

9   *El País*, 24 January, 1993, 5.
10 Kelly, *Labour and the Unions*, 10.
11 Rodrigues, "A Sindicalização da Classe Média", 3.
12 Ibid.
13 Bihr, *Du 'Grand Soir'*, 107.

of the working class. During the 1980s, it was possible to observe a decrease in strike action in advanced capitalist countries, due to the difficulties of bringing together, in the same company, workers with 'stability' and the ones who are 'outsourced', temporary, immigrants – segments that could not count, in a great measure, on a union representative. All this makes the possibilities to develop and consolidate a *class consciousness* among workers, based in feelings of *belonging to a class* more difficult. As a consequence, the risks of xenophobic, corporatist, racists and patronizing movements increase inside the world of work.[14]

This complex framework, with multiple tendencies and directions, deeply affected trade unionism, giving rise to the *most intense crisis* of its history. It struck advanced capitalist countries, particularly during the 1980s, but later, following the global dimension of these transformations, also hit countries in the Global South, especially those with significant industrialization, like Brazil, Mexico and many others. This trade unions' crisis is facing a scenario that, synthetically, has the following tendencies:

1) A growing individualization of work relations, displacing the axis of relations between labour and capital from the national sphere to economic sectors and from there to the *micro* dimension: the workplace, companies and within companies to increasingly *individualized* relations. This tendency consolidates in an essentially harmful element: enterprise trade unionism, 'house union', which originated in Toyota and nowadays is spread worldwide;

2) A very strong trend to deregulate and make labour markets flexible to their *limits*, deeply impacting historical achievements of trade unions, which until now were incapable of stopping these transformations.

3) The exhaustion in capitalist advanced countries of existing trade union models that chose, in this last decade and to a large degree, to adopt the *participatory trade unionism* line. Now they assess their huge losses, structural unemployment being the most evident of them, threatening to implode these same trade unions. As several strikes in the 1990s have shown, this (re)compels them, on a global scale, to once again struggle – in more audacious and in some cases more radical forms – to preserve some social rights and to reduce working hours as a possible way – in an immediate dimension – to decrease structural unemployment. When we mention the

---

14   Ibid., 107–108.

exhaustion of existing trade union models in capitalist advanced countries, we are thinking of their different versions, as synthesised by Freyssinet[15]:

a. The Anglo-Saxon model (similar to the North American model), which is characterized by government action influenced by neoliberal and ultraconservative trends, and by hostile employers aiming to undermine and even eliminate trade unions. Rights are constantly reduced and negotiation increasingly fragmented;

b. The German model, considered dual since it is based, on one side, on collective agreements linked to the respective professional fields and, on the other, to the attainment and exercise of limited but real management rights. This model, according to Freyssinet, presupposes the tripartite presence of the State, employers and trade unions, which despite their differences and conflicts agree to maintain the stability of the 'game's rules'.

c. The Japanese model, *participatory* and founded on the enterprise trade unionism. Linked to the corporations' culture and project, it gains, in return, certain guarantees of jobs and wages stability, as well as the right to be consulted on issues of work organisation.[16]

If it is true that, in the limits of this generalization, the German model is the one that is the least harmful to workers in core countries – deserving, therefore, greater attention from most of them – it is also clear that on capital's side, the preferred options oscillate between the English and the Japanese models.[17] Nevertheless, we think that with the crisis of the welfare state and the teardown of what was achieved during the social-democratic phase, it is not difficult to see the deadlock that this version of trade unionism faces. The *participatory path* links and subordinate trade unions' actions to the conditions imposed by the ruling classes, in the sense that it is limited to immediate demands and to what is agreed upon by capital. It has achieved extremely frail and even detrimental results when it takes into account the *entirety of the class-that-lives-from-labour*.

---

15   Jacques Freyssinet, "Syndicalismes en Europe", *Le Mouvement Social*, no. 162 (1993).
16   Ibid. In the same volume, Jelle Visser, discusses the alternatives for unions considering Europe's unification, offering the following characterization: the "german social-corporatist model, the English liberal-voluntarist and the French state-paternalistic". See Visser, "Syndicalisme et Désyndicalisation.".
17   Freyssinet, "Syndicalismes en Europe", 13–14.

This is the reason why alternative trade union movements started to be more expressive, questioning the prominently *defensive* action of traditional unions limited to action inside the order. To illustrate this, we can mention the *Cobas (Comitati di Base)*. It began to arise in mid-1980s in Italy, in sectors linked to public education, flight controllers, railway workers and even to some industrial workers. They sharply questioned agreements made by traditional federations of trade unions, especially CGIL – coming from a former communist tendency – that has, in general, guided their action by a moderate union policy.[18]

4) Growing trends of *bureaucratization* and *institutionalization* in unions, *distancing themselves from autonomous social movements* and choosing the alternative to act more and more integrated into an *institutional framework*. This results in unions gaining 'legitimacy' and a moderate status, due to their increasing distance from anticapitalistic actions and the loss of social radicalization. They were formed and consolidated themselves as *defensive organizations* and, therefore, have been unable to develop and trigger actions *beyond capital*.[19]

5) Alongside the rampant cult of individualism and social resignation, capital greatly expands – using more ideological and manipulative methods, rather than *direct* repression, reserved only for strictly necessary moments – its actions to insulate and curb left-wing movements, especially those with anticapitalistic practices. It is commonplace nowadays, in any part of the commodity-producing society, this *adverse and hostile* atmosphere against the left, against militant unions and social movements inspired by socialism.

If these are the ongoing trends, we want to conclude this part of our book, about the current dimensions of trade unions' crisis, indicating *some* of the enormous challenges facing *the unions movement as a whole*, on a global scale

---

18 Detailed information and a critical analysis about Cobas can be found in Lorenzo Bordogna, "'Arcipelago Cobas': Frammentazione della rappresentanza e conflitti di Lavoro", in *Política in Italia* (Bologna: Mulino Publisher, 1988), p. 257–292.

19 István Mészáros, "Marxism Today: an Interview with István Mészáros", interview by Chris Arthur and Joseph McCarney, *Monthly Review*, vol. 39/3 (1993), 20–21; *A Necessidade do Controle Social* (São Paulo: Ensaio, 1989), 114. João Bernardo took this criticism to the extreme showing, with certain reason, that unions became also large capitalist enterprises, acting under a logic that is not different from private companies. See João Bernardo, *Capital, Sindicatos, Gestores* (São Paulo: Vértice, 1987).

and at the end of the 20th century. We can sum up part of these challenges, as the following:

1) Will trade unions be capable of breaking the huge social barrier that separates the workers with 'stability' – more 'integrated' into the production process, and quantitatively decreasing – from the ones who are part-time, precarious, 'outsourced', informal, whose numbers are significantly expanding in the contemporary production process? Will they be capable of *organising the unorganised workers in trade unions* and, therefore, reverse the decreasing unionisation rates of the main capitalist societies?
2) Will unions be capable of stopping *neo-corporatism*, which exclusively defends their respective professions and abandons or strongly diminishes more prominent class content? Here, as mentioned earlier, we are dealing with *social corporatism*: exclusionary, partial, *preserving* and even *intensifying* the fragmented and heterogeneous character of the working class. Will they be capable of emphatically refusing the actions of the more backward sectors – which sometimes get closer to xenophobic, ultranationalist and racist movements that are responsible for actions against immigrant workers from the Global South – and, instead, forge solidary and classist forms of actions, capable of integrating workers practically excluded even from the unions' representation?
3) Will they be capable of reversing the trend – developed from Toyotism and nowadays expanding worldwide – to reduce unions exclusively to the factory's scope, to the so-called *enterprise trade unionism* and *involvement trade unionism*, more vulnerable and subordinated to employers' orders? As we have already shown, the main space for professional relations to act was displaced from the national dimension to economic sectors and from there to companies and workplaces. This reallocation of power and initiative to the businesses' universe harmed unions and public institutions, as is recognised by OECD's Annual Report itself (1992). Will unions be capable of stopping capital's tendency to *reduce trade unionism to the enterprises' universe, to this microcosm that individualizes and personalizes the relation between capital and labour?* Will they be able to (re)organize the factories' committees and autonomous organizations in the workplace capable of inhibiting capital's tendency to co-opt workers?
4) Will they be capable of creating a *horizontal trade unionism*, better equipped to integrate the totality of the *class-that-lives-from-labour*,

overcoming therefore the *vertical trade unionism* that predominated since Fordism, which have been incapable of assimilating both the new ranks of wageworkers and the ones *without jobs*?

5) Will they be capable of breaking with the growing trend of excessive *institutionalization and bureaucratization* that has heavily marked unions on a global scale and pulled them away from their social bases, further deepening the abyss between unions and autonomous social movements?

6) Respecting their specificities, will trade unions be capable of going beyond their very *defensive* actions and, therefore, *assist* the quest for a more ambitious project towards workers' emancipation? Will unions be able to rescue actions aimed at *controlling social production*, instead of losing themselves *exclusively* in the field of phenomenic and immediate actions that do not even minimally question capital's order and the commodity-producing system?

To these questions, we can add those which are *specific* to unions in industrialized and intermediate industrializing countries in Latin America, like Brazil, Mexico, Argentina, Venezuela, Chile, as well as in recently industrialized Asian countries like Korea, Hong Kong, Taiwan, Singapore and many others. Will unions be capable of hindering the generalization of this *trade unions' crisis*, which already struck them, with more or less intensity? Will the more militant unions that exist in several of these countries, be capable of participating and assisting in the making of an *alternative economic model*? A model with clear anticapitalistic characteristics which, at the same time, is fundamentally based on technological development with a real and national base, instead of ruled by the logic of a destructive and exclusionary commodity-producing system, responsible for the explosive structural unemployment rates, nowadays spread worldwide? As it is possible to see, these are some of the challenges which will define the future of unions at the end of 20th century.

In this sense, in presenting the challenges we consider more urgent to trade unions, we tried to offer an analytical framework of their world scale *crisis*. The paths unions follow will be, for sure, capable of avoiding their disappearance as workers' representative bodies, at least in the foreseeable future. However, it is not yet clearly delineated whether these actions will be able or not to *block* the tendencies that increasingly undermine and wear unions out.

CHAPTER 4

Which Crisis of Labour Society?

What we previously analysed allows us to indicate some 'thesis' in order to offer conclusions on the topics developed in this book.[1]

1   First Thesis

In contrast to the authors who defend the category of labour loss of centrality in contemporary society, ongoing trends either towards a greater intellectualization of factory work and the increase in skilled labour, or in the direction of deskilling and subproletarianization, do not allow us to reach this conclusion in the universe of a *commodity-producing society*. Even if there is a quantitative reduction (with qualitative repercussions) in the world of production, *abstract labour* plays a decisive role in the creation of exchange values. Commodities generated in the world of capital are results of the activity (manual and/or intellectual) of human labour interacting with means of production. The "diminution of the subjective factor of the labour process as compared with the objective factor" or "the increase of the constant constituent of capital at the expense of its variable constituent" relatively decreases the role of *collective labour* in the production of exchange values, but do not eliminate it.[2] Products created by Toyota, Benetton or Volvo, for instance, are not anything other than *commodities* that result from the interaction between *living* and *dead labour*, variable capital and constant capital.

Even in a technologically developed production process (where one could witness the prevalence of more intellectualized, more skilled activities), the creation of exchange values would still be the result of this *articulation* between *living* and *dead labour*. It seems difficult to imagine it differently when the commodity-producing system is considered on a global scale. The reduction of physical labour time in the production process, as well as the reduction of direct manual labour and the expansion of more intellectualized labour do *not invalidate the law of value*, when it is considered the *totality of*

---

1 Since this book is a result of ongoing research, it becomes evident that despite the predominantly affirmative character of these 'thesis' they are subjected to review and transformations.
2 Karl Marx, "Capital. Volume 1: The Process of Production of Capital", in *Karl Marx & Friedrich Engels, Collected Works, vol. 35* (London: Lawrence & Wishart, 1996), 617–618.

labour, the capacity of socially combined work, the collective worker as an expression of multiple *activities combined*.

When we consider the crisis of labour society, it seems decisive to remember the Marxian distinction between *concrete* and *abstract labour*:

> on the one hand, all labour is, speaking physiologically, an expenditure of human labour power, and in its character of identical abstract human labour, it creates and forms the value of commodities. On the other hand, all labour is the expenditure of human labour power in a special form and with a definite aim, and in this, its character of concrete useful labour, it produces use values.[3]

On one side, there is the *useful* character of labour, the exchange between humans and nature, a condition to produce *socially useful and necessary things*. This is the moment when *concrete labour* is realized, labour in its qualitative dimension. Apart from this useful character of labour – this *concrete* dimension – what remains is only the fact that it is an expenditure of socially determined human productive force – physical or intellectual. Here arises its *abstract* dimension, in which it is "put out of sight [...] the useful character of the various kinds of labour", and in which "there is nothing left but what is common to them all; all are reduced to one and the same sort of labour, human labour in the abstract".[4]

It is known that in the universe of the commodity-producing sociability – which has the creation of exchange values as its basic goal – use values are minimized, reduced and subsumed to their exchange values. They are considered only as a *necessary* condition to realize capital's valorisation process, in the commodity-producing system.[5] As a result, labour's *concrete* dimension is also entirely subordinated to its *abstract* one. Therefore, when one speaks

---

3 Ibid., 56.
4 Ibid., 48.
5 It was exploring this tendency that István Mészáros developed the thesis about the *decreasing rate of utilization* in capitalism: "Capital treats *use-value* (which directly corresponds to need) and *exchange value* not merely as separate, but in a way that radically subordinates the former to the latter [...] in its own time and place this represents a radical innovation that opens up formerly unimaginable horizons for economic development. An innovation based on the practical realization that any particular commodity may be constantly in use, at one end of the scale, or indeed never be used at all, at the other extreme of the possible rates of utilization, without losing thereby its usefulness as regards the expansionary requirements of the capitalist mode of production". István Mészáros, *Beyond Capital: Towards a Theory of Transition* (London: Merlin Press, 1995), 566–567.

about the crisis of labour society, it is absolutely necessary to qualify which dimension one is referring to: if it is a crisis of *abstract* labour (as Robert Kurz suggests[6]) or also a crisis of its *concrete* dimension, as a structuring element of social exchange between humans and nature (as suggests Offe, Gorz and Habermas, among many others[7]).

In the first case, which refers to the crisis of *abstract* labour, there is a distinction that seems decisive to us and, in general, has been neglected. *The essential point here is this: is the contemporary society predominantly moved or not by capital's logic, by the commodity-producing system?* If the answer is affirmative, the crisis of *abstract* labour can only be understood, in Marxian terms, as a *reduction* of living labour and an expansion of dead labour. We agree with Kurz on this point, when he says that:

> the *labour society* as an ontological concept would be a tautology, since in history social life thus far, in whichever modified form it assumes, could only be a life that included labour. Only naïve ideas of the paradise and wonderland tales fantasize about a society without labour.[8]

In this case, however, it is possible to observe at least two very distinct ways to understand the so-called *crisis of abstract labour society*: the first – to which we have already shown our disagreement – thinks the labouring being does not play a structuring role anymore in the creation of exchange values, in the creation of commodities; and the second criticizes the abstract labour society because it assumes the form of *alienated, fetishized* labour that *de-realizes* autonomous human activity. In this second interpretation, which apprehends capitalism's essentiality, the central role of the working class in creating exchange values is recognized – naturally taking into account all discussions we have made in the previous chapters. However, this recognition emphasizes that this labour *form of being* in the commodity realm is, as Marx has shown since the *1844 Manuscripts*, essentially harmful to the social being, who strives for *omnilaterality* but experiences *unilaterality* under the form of alienated

---

6 Robert Kurz, *O Colapso da Modernização: Da Derrocada do Socialismo de Caserna à Crise da Economia Mundial* (São Paulo: Paz e Terra, 1992).

7 Claus Offe, "Trabalho como Categoria Sociológica Fundamental?", *Trabalho & Sociedade*, vol. 1 (1989); André Gorz, *Farewell to the Working Class: an Essay on Post-Industrial Socialism* (London: Pluto Press, 1982); "The New Agenda", *New Left Review*, no. 184 (1990); Jürgen Habermas, "The New Obscurity", in *The New Conservatism: Cultural Criticism and the Historians' Debate* (Cambridge: Polity Press, 1989).

8 Kurz, *O Colapso da Modernização*, 26.

labour. Here it is *strongly rejected the cult of wage labour*, heavily idealized by various Marxist streams in the 20th century. Contemporary sociability, more *fetishist* than earlier epochs, reaffirms and intensifies *alienated* labour and the destructive logic of the commodity-producing system.

Most advocates of the other critical trend, the one that denies the capitalist character of contemporary society, refuse labour's central role in its *abstract* dimension, as creator of exchange values, since this would be no longer decisive nowadays. Furthermore, they also deny *concrete* labour's role in shaping a meaningful life and structuring an emancipated world. Characterized either as a service, post-industrial and post-capitalist society, or by a tripartite institutional logic, resulting from a pact between capital, workers and the State, this contemporary society, less market based and more contractual, would no longer be centrally ruled by capital's logic. Instead, it is marked by the social subject's search for alterity, by comprehensive relations based on citizenship, by an expansion of 'non-commodified zones', or by the dispute of public funds.[9]

Habermas presents the most articulated synthesis of this interpretation:

> the utopia of a labour society lost its persuasive force [...] Above all, the utopian idea of a labouring society of independent producers has lost its persuasive power [...] Above all, it is because that utopian idea has lost its point of reference in reality: the power of abstract labour to give structure and form to a society. Claus Offe has compiled convincing "indications of an objectively decreasing power of the factors of labour, production, and

---

9 From what we have formulated previously, we cannot agree also with the always creative and thought-provoking Francisco de Oliveira when he claims – despite the several differences with the authors mentioned above, especially his recognition of class struggles, which is not secondary in his analysis – that the pattern of public financing of the *welfare state* "undertook a real 'Copernican revolution' in the fundaments of value category as the core of the reproduction both of capital and labour power. Taken to its limits, the pattern of public financing 'imploded' value as the only presupposition of capital's extended reproduction, partially dissolving it as measure of economic activity and sociability in general". See Francisco de Oliveira, "O Surgimento do Anti-Valor", *Novos Estudos Cebrap*, no. 22 (1988), 13–14. What seems relevant to us here is to question which one of them – value or public fund – has the status of foundation of contemporary sociability, in the process of capital's reproduction. The crisis of *welfare state*, the neoliberal landslide and the global dimension of capital can confirm the predominance of value as the structuring element of the commodity-producing sociability and the public fund as being its regulator/counterpoint and *not its substitute* – and there is a huge difference here. Francisco de Oliveira's formulation, made in an embryonic way, developed in a later text to a "theoretical and conceptual elaboration" of a "social-democratic mode of production" that articulates value and anti-value. See Francisco de Oliveira, "A Economia Política da Social-Democracia", *Revista USP*, no. 136 (1992).

profit in determining the state of a society and societal development in general".[10]

After referring favourably to Gorz's work, Habermas adds:

> the utopian core, deliverance from heteronomous labour, has clearly taken on another form within the project of the social welfare state. Emancipated living conditions worthy of human beings are no longer seen as arising directly from a revolution in working conditions, that is, from a transformation of heteronomous Labour into self-directed activity.[11]

Although Habermas indicates labour's *abstract* dimension here, it is evident that in this interpretative trend labour no longer has a structuring potential, either in contemporary society's universe, as *abstract* labour, or as fundament of a "utopia of a labouring society", as *concrete* labour, since the "utopian accents shift from the concept of labour to that of communication".[12]

We believe that when one says *farewell to work* without properly incorporating the distinction between *concrete* and *abstract* labour, a strong analytical mistake is made, since the double dimension of the phenomenon is conflated into one. It is suggestive to recall A. Heller when she says work must be apprehended in its double aspect: as a performance which is *part of everyday life* and as a *work-activity*, a species-being objectivation. Heller says Marx often uses two different words to better characterize work's double dimension: *work* and *labour*. The former often refers to the *concrete* activity that creates socially useful values; the latter frequently express a daily alienated performance.[13] *Work*,

---

10   Habermas, "The New Obscurity", 4.
11   Ibid., 5. In a more empirical way, but essentially converging with this thesis, A. Touraine says: "the problems of labour have not disappeared, but they are encompassed by a larger whole. As such, they do not represent a central role anymore. It is useless to search for signs of a revolutionary renovation based specifically in workers. In the places where workers movement apparently is more militant, as in Italy and France, they gain, little by little, and through conflicts and crisis that can be violent, broader rights and bargain capacity. Therefore, a certain institutionalization of labour conflicts [...] Workers cease to be a central character in social history, as we approach a post-industrial society". And Gorz, close to Touraine, adds that other social antagonisms were imposed over the ones unleashed by capital and labour, which were relativized and even overcome by the 'central conflict' between the 'bureaucratic–industrial megamachine' and the population. See Alain Touraine, "Os Novos Conflitos Sociais", *Lua Nova*, no. 17 (1989); Gorz, "The New Agenda", 42.
12   Habermas, "The New Obscurity", 16.
13   Agnes Heller, *Everyday Life* (London: Routledge & Kegan Paul, 1984), 60–70.

therefore, refers to a species-being activity that transcends daily life. It is the dimension of use values production, where the *concrete* character of praxis prevails. In contrast, *labour* often refers to a daily performance that, under capitalism, takes the form of an e*stranged, fetishized activity*. To neglect this double dimension of work makes it possible to mistakenly interpret the crisis of abstract labour society as a crisis of the concrete labour society.

The sublation of abstract labour society, under the terms we are suggesting here, is conditioned to the recognition of the central role played by wage labour, by the *class-that-lives-from-labour*, as the subject potentially capable of, objectively and subjectively, *going beyond capital*.[14] *Therefore, this is a crisis of the abstract labour society and its sublation has the working class as the central point – even as fragmented, heterogeneous and complex as it currently is*. And there is, as previously indicated, another consequence when the double dimension of the labouring act is neglected: the rejection of labour's role as a *proto-form* of emancipated human activity. The *concrete* role of labour is negated as the *first* moment in the realization of an omnilateral individuality, a condition without which the *species-being-for-itself* cannot be realized.

Here an instigating question emerges: the sublation of the abstract labour society (to use this expression again) and the transition to an emancipated society founded on concrete labour presupposes the reduction of working hours and the expansion of free time. *Simultaneously, it also presupposes a radical transformation of alienated labour into social labour as the source and base of human emancipation, of omnilateral consciousness.* In other words, the radical refusal of abstract labour should not lead to reject the possibility of conceiving concrete labour as the primary, original dimension or the starting point to realize social and human needs. It is the non-acceptance of this thesis that takes many authors, Gorz at the forefront, to imagine labour as *always heteronomous*. What remains, in this perspective, is only the struggle for liberated time: the realization of *labour that demeans and time (outside labour) that sets free*. This actually is the utopian and romantic idea since it disregards the overarching and totalizing dimension of capital, ranging from the production sphere to that of consumption, from the material plan to the world of ideas.[15]

---

14 This seems to be one of the mistakes in Kurz's thought-provoking book, which recognizes the commodity-producing society, but ends up believing in the thesis of the extinction of the working class, as the subject capable to push these transformations.

15 Berman's comments about intellectual and aesthetic work under capitalism – perhaps too directly and suppressing several *mediations*, but for sure apprehending the essential – describes in this way the determinations of those kind of works: intellectuals in capitalism "can write books, paint pictures, discover physical or historical laws, save lives, only if someone with capital will pay them. But the pressures of bourgeois society are such that

We understand that the action effectively capable of making the leap *beyond capital* possible will be the one that integrates demands from daily life into the world of work – like the *radical* reduction of working hours and the striving for 'free time' under capitalism – *as long as this action is necessarily linked to the end of abstract labour society and its conversion into a society that creates truly useful things*. This will be the starting point of a *social organization directed to fulfilment in the realm of necessities (the sphere where labour is) and from there to the realm of freedom (the sphere where labour ceases to be determined, as Marx said, by the necessity and utility externally imposed)*.[16] This is a *condition of a project founded upon the free association of individuals that became effectively social*, where there is an identity between the individual and human kind.

When the labour movement constrains itself and sticks *exclusively* to the struggle to reduce working hours, this action constitutes an extremely defensive and insufficient position, limited to acting inside the commodity-producing society. It is crucial to articulate the more immediate struggles with an alternative and global project of a social organization, founded on a logic where production of exchange value does not find *any* possibility of becoming the structuring element.

The possible solution, therefore, is the

> general adoption and creative utilization of *disposable time* as the orienting principle of societal reproduction [...] from the standpoint of living labour; it is perfectly possible to envisage disposable time as the condition that fulfils some vital positive functions in the life-activity of the associated producers (functions which it alone can fulfil), provided that the lost unity between need and production is reconstituted at a qualitatively higher level than it ever existed in the historical relationship between 'the snail and its shell' [the worker and means of production].[17]

---

no one will pay them unless it pays to pay them – that is, unless their works somehow help to 'increase capital'. They must 'sell themselves piecemeal' to an employer willing to exploit their brains for profit. They must scheme and hustle to present themselves in a maximally profitable light; they must compete (often brutally and unscrupulously) for the privilege of being bought, simply in order to go on with their work. Once the work is done they are, like all other workers, separated from the products of their labour. Their goods and services go on sale, and it is 'the vicissitudes of competition, the fluctuations of the market', rather than any intrinsic truth or beauty or value [...] that will determine their fate". Marshall Berman, *All that is Solid Melts into Air* (London: Penguin Books, 1988), 117.

16   Karl Marx, "Capital. Volume 3: *The Process of Capitalist Production as a Whole*", in *Karl Marx & Friedrich Engels, Collected Works, vol. 37* (London: Lawrence & Wishart, 1998), 807.

17   Mészáros, *Beyond Capital*, 573–574.

Disposable time, from the point of view of the labour that produces socially useful and necessary things, will enable the elimination of all *surplus labour* accumulated by capital and used in the destructive production of exchange values. In this way, *disposable time* controlled by labour, producing use values – and, consequently, restoring labour's *concrete* dimension, while dissolving its *abstract* one – will be able to establish a social logic radically different from the commodity-producing society. Once again, this will be capable of bringing to the forefront the foundational role of *creative labour*, which supresses the distinction between manual and intellectual labour – base of the social division of labour under capital – and can, therefore, constitute itself as the *proto-form* of an emancipated human activity.

2 Second Thesis

Since social labour is the creator of *use values*, of useful things, the form of exchange between nature and the social being, it does not seem plausible to conceive, in the universe of human sociability, its extinction. If it is possible to visualize the elimination of *abstract* labour society – what is, naturally, linked to the end of commodity-producing society – something ontologically distinct is to suppose or conceive of the end of *labour* as a useful activity, as life-activity, as the foundational element, *proto-form* of human activity. In other words: it is one thing to conceive, *with the elimination of capitalism*, the end of *abstract labour*, of *alienated* labour; another, very distinct, is to conceive the elimination, in the universe of human sociability, of *concrete labour*, which creates socially useful things and, in doing so, transforms its own creator. If one considers labour as devoid of this *double* dimension, what is left is to assume that it is synonymous with *abstract, alienated and fetishized labour*.[18] Therefore, the consequence that unfolds from this is, in the best hypothesis, to imagine a society of *free time*, with some meaning, alongside the existing forms of *alienated* and *fetishized* labour.

This *second thesis* – which unfolds from the previous one – is, therefore, an outcome of not taking into account labour's double character, as it happens in

---

18   André Gorz does not escape from this analytical limitation: "*work* has not always existed in the way in which it is currently understood. It came into being at the same time as capitalists and proletarians". From there, Gorz says " 'work' nowadays refers almost exclusively to activities carried out for a wage. The terms 'work' and 'job' have become interchangeable [...]". Gorz, *Farewell to the Working Class*, 9.

many critiques of the so-called labouring society. Labour, as a creator of use value, as useful labour,

> is a necessary condition, independent of all forms of society, for the existence of the human race; it is an eternal nature-imposed necessity, without which there can be no material exchanges between man and Nature, and therefore no life.[19]

In this species-being dimension, labour has an essential meaning in the universe of human sociability. As Lukács says:

> only with labour does its ontological nature give it a pronounced transitional character. It is by its very nature a relationship of interchange between man (society) and nature, and moreover with inorganic nature [...] as well as organic, and although this relationship can also figure in at certain points in the series just indicated, it characterizes above all of the transition in the working man himself from purely biological being to social being.[20]

This is why labour is considered, therefore, as the 'model', an 'original phenomenon', *proto-form* of the social being.[21] The simple fact that in labour a teleological position is realized, configures it as an elemental experience of daily life, becoming an inseparable component of the social being. This enables Lukács to claim that the *genesis of the social being, its separation from its original basis and also its transformation are based on labour, that is, on the continuous realization of teleological positions.*[22]

In this species-being dimension, as human self-activity, creator of useful things, work has a central ontological status in *social praxis*:

---

19 Marx, "Capital. Volume 1", 53. This conception, essential to Marx, reappears almost literally in chapter VII of *Capital*, where the labour process is discussed. We disagree, therefore, with a text written by Agnes Heller – in the early 1980s, already marked by her break with the old Lukács – *reinterpreting* fundamental elements of the Marxian formulation, and attributing to *Capital* and its preparatory studies the prevalence of a "paradigm of production", which differs from a "paradigm of work" that exists in the *1844 Manuscripts*. Agnes Heller, "Paradigma dela Produzione e Paradigma del Lavoro", *Critica Marxista*, no. 4 (1981), 103–105.
20 György Lukács, *The Ontology of Social Being: 3. Labour* (London: Merlin Press, 1980), iv.
21 Ibid., v.
22 Ibid.

we may rightly call the working man [...] a responding being. There is no doubt that all work emerges as a solution in response to necessity. [...] we become responding beings by fact that [...] we formulate in questions our necessities, and determine the means available to satisfy them. It is in answer to these necessities that we ground and enlarge our activity through the manifold of mediations. Thus, not only the answer but also the question is the product of the consciousness that governs this activity. Nevertheless, the answering does not cease to be ontologically primary in this moving complex. Material necessity, as the moving force of the individual and social reproduction processes, really sets in motion first labour with its complexity [...] Only when labour becomes completely dominated by mankind, only when it already encompasses the possibility of being 'not merely a means for survival' but the first requirement of life, only when mankind has passed beyond every constraint of self-reproduction, only then will the social path be cleared for human activity as an end in itself.[23]

Here, once again, clearly appears the greatest fragility of labouring society critics: the disregard of the essential dimension of concrete labour, as the foundation (insofar as it is inserted in the necessities sphere) able to make possible the material basis on which the other spheres of human activities can develop themselves. In truth, the perspective of labouring society critics is founded on the recognition and acceptance that labour ruled by the logic of commodities and capital is inevitable, resulting in the assumption that human work cannot become a real self-activity.

It is important to reassert that labour, understood as the *proto-form* of human activity, cannot be confused with an *exclusive and totalizing moment*; instead, what we are trying to retain here is that the concrete labour sphere is the *starting point* under which it will be possible to establish a new society. The moment of human omnilaterality (that has art, ethics, philosophy, science, etc. as more elevated forms) evidently transcends, to a great deal, the sphere of labour (the satisfaction of needs), but has to find in it its basis.

In this sense, automation, robotics, microelectronics, in sum the so-called technological revolution has an evident emancipatory meaning, *as long as it is not ruled by the destructive logic of the commodity-producing system, but by*

---

23   György Lukács, "The 'Vienna Paper': The Ontological Foundations of Human Thinking and Action", in *Lukács's Last Autocriticism: the Ontology*, ed. Ernst Joós (Atlantic Highlands: Humanities Press, 1982), 138–139; 147.

the society of disposable time, producer of socially useful and necessary goods. In Mandel's synthesis:

> Marx opposes the emancipatory potential of automation and robotism – its capacity to greatly increase the amount of human leisure time, time for full development of the all-round personality – to its oppressive tendency under capitalism. He synthesises this opposition precisely as being that between a class society and a classless society.[24]

He, then, adds:

> in a class society, appropriation of the social surplus by a minority means capacity of extending leisure time for only a minority, and therefore reproduction on a larger and larger scale of the division of society between those who administer and accumulate knowledge, and those who produce without or with only very limited knowledge. In a classless society, appropriation and control of the social surplus product by all (by the associated producers) would mean a radical reduction of labour time (of necessary labour) for all, a radical extension of leisure for all, and thereby the disappearance of the division of society between administrators and producers, between those who have access to all knowledge and those who are cut off from most knowledge.[25]

The critics of the labouring society, with some honourable exceptions, 'empirically observe' *abstract* labour's loss of relevance in modern society – turned 'post-industrial' and 'services' society – and consequently, they deduce and generalize from that observation, the 'end of labouring society's utopia', in its broad and general sense.[26]

---

24 Ernst Mandel, "Marx, the Present Crisis and the Future of Labour", *Socialist Register*, vol. 22 (1985–1986), 444.
25 Ibid.
26 Although close to Habermas and Gorz when it comes to the world of work's loss of centrality in contemporary society, Robert Kurz significantly diverges from them when he emphasizes, as we showed previously, the end of *abstract* labour society. Kurz, *O Colapso da Modernização*. Differently, Offe says "[...] one can talk about a crisis of labouring society in the sense that signs accumulate showing formal paid labour lost its subjective quality as the organizing core of human activities, of self-esteem and social references, as well as of moral guidance. [...] the quality of a worker becomes inappropriate to found the identity – and therefore also to a uniform sociological interpretation of interests and consciousness – of those who *are* workers". Offe, "Trabalho como Categoria Sociológica

Suggesting a different direction we tried to indicate here that these formulations have vast limitations (that on a large measure result from the neglect of Marxian analytical categories), which the greatest example is the disregard of the double dimension of labour/work (as *abstract* labour and *concrete* labour). When the defence of market and capital society is not clearly clarified in these formulations, what remains is the utopian and romantic proposition of *free time* inside a fetishized society, as if it was possible to live an *absolutely meaningless life* in labour and a *meaningful one outside it*. Or, repeating what we said before, trying to reconcile *demeaning labour* with *liberated time*.[27]

3   Third Thesis

Although *heterogeneous, complex and fragmented* as labour currently is, the possibilities of an effective human emancipation can still find social concreteness and viability through revolts and rebellions which originate *centrally* in the world of work; a process of emancipation simultaneously *from* work and *for* work. These rebellions and revolts neither *exclude* nor *suppress* other forms of defiance and contestation. However, living in a society that produces exchange values, labour's revolts have a central status. All the broad range of wageworkers in the service sector, 'outsourced', informal, working from home, unemployed, sub-employed, etc. suffer heavily with the social demolition put forward by capitalism and its destructive logic. They can (and should) join the directly productive workers; acting as a *class* they constitute themselves as the social segment endowed with the greatest *anticapitalistic* potential.

In sum, the *class-that-lives-from-labour* is central to transformations that goes in the opposite direction of the logic of capital accumulation and the commodity-producing system. As the contemporary world has abundantly shown, other types of social struggle (such as the ecologic, feminist, anti-racist, LGBT, youth, etc.) have great importance for pursuing an individuality and a sociability full of meaning. However, when the *axis* is the *resistance and confrontation against capital's logic and the commodity-producing society*, the centre of this action finds greater *radicalization* when it is developed and amplified

---

Fundamental?", 7–8. In this case, the conceptual universe is very different from the one used by Robert Kurz.

27   Or, according to a *hybrid* formulation – in the end also subordinated to the logic given by capital's economic rationality – "socialism must be conceived as the binding of capitalist rationality within a democratically planned framework, which should serve the achievement of democratically determined goals [...]". Gorz, "The New Agenda", 46.

inside the working class – although, it is recognized that this enterprise is much more complex and harder than it was in the past, when workers' fragmentation and heterogeneity did not have the intensity that it has nowadays.

The central element that sustains our formulation is, therefore, the reassertion that the commodity-producing system is working on a global scale. Hence, as Mészáros states:

> the understanding of the development and self-reproduction of the capitalist mode of production is quite impossible without the concept of the *total* social capital, which alone can explain many mysteries of the commodity society – from the 'average rate of profit' to the laws governing capital expansion and concentration. Similarly, it is quite impossible to understand the manifold and thorny problems of nationally varied as well as socially stratified labour without constantly keeping in mind the necessary framework of a proper assessment: namely the irreconcilable antagonism between *total* social capital and the *totality* of labour. This fundamental antagonism, going without saying, is inevitably modified in accordance with: a) the local social-economic circumstances; b) the respective positions of particular countries in the global framework of capital production; and c) the relative maturity of the global social-historical development.[28]

Although it results from a heterogeneous labouring activity, socially combined and globally articulated, the *totality of labour* fulfils its central role in the process that creates exchange values. If, to this element, we add other points of contradiction, coming from the capital's production process itself – such as the huge number of unemployed, linked to the explosive structural unemployment

---

28   István Mészáros, *The Necessity of Social Control* (New York: Monthly Review Press, 2015), 46. This intensification of social contradictions is pointed out also by Octávio Ianni, when he claims that "[…] under global capitalism social contradictions also become global, i.e., they generalize themselves more than ever. Their social, economic, political and cultural components develop themselves around the world. What previously was an uneven and combined development in the scope of each national society and each imperialist system, now under world capitalism becomes universal. The unevenness, tensions and contradictions generalize themselves in the regional, national, continental and global scope, encompassing social classes, ethnical groups, minorities, cultures, religions and other expressions of the world kaleidoscope. Various expressions of diversity are transformed in inequalities, markers, stigmas, forms of alienation, conditions to protest, base to struggles for emancipation […]. Therefore, the social question, that some sectors of dominant countries imagined as overcome, resurge with other data, colours and meanings". Octávio Ianni, *A Sociedade Global* (Rio de Janeiro: Civilização Brasileira, 1992), 143–144.

rates on a global scale – we will find here, *due to the set of social beings which depend on selling their labour power*, a large part of possible actions aiming *beyond capital*. That is why we do not agree with the thesis that defends that class actions disappeared and lost their anticapitalistic potential. The revolution of our days is, in this sense, a revolution *in* labour and *of* labour. It is a revolution *in* labour, in the sense that it necessarily has to *abolish* abstract, wage labour, the condition of the commodity-subject, and establish a society based on human self-activity, on concrete labour that generates socially useful things, on emancipated social labour. But it is also a revolution *of* labour, since it finds in the broad range of individuals (men and women) that belong to the working class the *collective subject* capable of promoting actions in an emancipatory direction.

4 Fourth Thesis

The more heterogeneous, complex and fragmented character of the *class-that-lives-from-labour* does not indicate its extinction; contrary to a *farewell to work or to the working class*, the discussion that seems relevant to us is the one that recognizes, on one side, the *possibility* to emancipate *from* and *through* labour, as the decisive *starting point* to strive for human omnilaterality. On the other hand, there is a huge challenge that comes from a complex social being ranging from sectors with greater skills – represented by those that were privileged by technological development and experienced an increased intellectualization of their work – to those that are part of precarious, partial, 'outsourced', informal labour, or the *subclass* of workers. We do not believe this heterogeneity makes it impossible for those social segments to act together, as a *class*, even if the approximation, articulation, and unification of these strata which form the working class are a much bigger challenge than imagined by the socialist left.[29]

From what was said above derives another interesting question, of enormous importance: in the workers' struggle and the struggle of the socially excluded ones that the world has witnessed and has some anticapitalistic dimension, is it possible to detect a greater *potentiality* and even *centrality* in the more qualified segments of the working class? Does this hold true for the ones that experience a more 'stable' situation and consequently have a greater participation in the value creation process? Or, differently, does the more fruitful

---

29   See Mészáros' considerations about labour fragmentation due to the social division of labour under capital, in "The Division of Labour and the Post-Capitalist State", *Monthly Review*, vol. 37/3 (1987), especially the item *The Division of Labour*.

anticapitalistic action comes from more excluded social segments, from the sub-proletarianized strata?

We do not believe this question can be completely answered nowadays. The metamorphoses were (and continue to be) of such an intensity that any answer would be premature. What seems more important to us is to emphasize the imperative need that these segments constituting the heterogeneous working class accept the challenge to strive for the necessary mechanisms capable of making a *class* confluence possible, against all the tendencies to individualize work relations, to exacerbate neo-corporatism, to accentuate contradictions inside the world of work, etc.

It is possible, nevertheless, to make a second remark about this question: those more skilled, intellectualized segments that developed themselves alongside technological improvement, due to the central role they play in the process of creating exchange values, could have, at least objectively, a greater anticapitalistic potential.[30] However, contradictorily, these more skilled sectors are exactly those that have experienced, subjectively, a greater 'integrative' involvement with capital – the attempts of manipulation elaborated by *Toyotism* being the best expression of it, very often responsible for actions based on conceptions inspired by *neo-corporatism*.

On the other hand, the broad range of precarious, partial, temporary, etc. workers, that we called *subproletariat*, alongside the huge numbers of unemployed, would have, on the material plan, a smaller relevance in anticapitalistic struggles, due to their distance (or even exclusion) from the value creation process. However, their dispossessed and excluded condition potentially place them as a social subject capable of taking more audacious action, *since these social segments do not have anything else to lose* in the world of capital's sociability. Their subjectivity could be, therefore, more inclined to rebel.

The recent strikes and social explosions in advanced capitalist countries mix elements of both of these poles of the 'dual society'. Therefore, we understand that overcoming capital can only be a result of an enterprise that brings together and articulates the diverse segments of the *class-that-lives-from-labour*.

For us, not recognizing this point is another of Gorz's mistakes. His emphasis on seeing the pole that is potentially capable of transforming society in the universe of the *non-class of non-workers* has, on one side, the merit of localizing anticapitalistic potentialities in this social segment. Although, the fact

---

30   Serge Mallet, two decades ago, developed the thesis that, because it was located at the core of the most developed productive complexes, the *new working class* would apprehend the system's contradiction poles before the traditional segments of the working class. Serge Mallet, *The New Working Class* (Nottingham: Spokesman Books, 1973), 29.

has a negative side, it understands productive workers as almost irreversibly integrated into capital's order, losing the possibility of seeing themselves as subjects capable of struggling for an emancipated life. This characterization also suffers from the conceptual error of naming an important and growing segment of the working class as *non-class of non-workers*.[31] As analysed previously, the *heterogeneity, fragmentation and complexification* take place inside the world of work, which ranges from productive workers, with 'stability', to the group of precarious workers, those experiencing structural unemployment, etc. It is those segments altogether, which depend on selling their labour power, that form the *totality of social labour*, the working class and the world of work.

5 Fifth Thesis

Capitalism in any of its contemporary variations – from the Swedish to the Japanese, or from the German to the North American experiences – was not capable, as we could indicate previously, of eliminating the multiple forms and expressions of *alienation* and, in many cases, there was even a process of its intensification and greater internalization – in the sense that it *minimizes* the dimension, inherent to Fordism, more explicitly despotic and stimulates the 'manipulatory involvement' of the age of Toyotism. If *alienation* is understood as the existence of social barriers opposing the development of individuality towards human omnilaterality, then the capitalism of our days at the same time that it, with advances in technology, potentializes human capacities, also enables the growing emergence of the social phenomenon of *alienation*. This is because the development of human capacities does not necessarily produces the development of an individuality full of meaning, but, on the contrary, "can disfigure, demean, etc. human personality", since technological development

---

31 For André Gorz, the *non-class of non-workers* "prefigures the future world. The abolition of work can have no other social subject than this non-class". Or, according to another passage: "the realm of freedom can never arise out of material processes; it can only be established by a constitutive act which, aware of its free subjectivity, asserts itself as an absolute end in itself within each individual. Only the non-class of non-producers is capable of such an act. For it alone embodies what lies beyond productivism: the rejection of the accumulation ethic and the dissolution of all classes". Gorz, *Farewell to the Working Class*, 7; 74. For who wrote a chapter entitled *The Working Class According to Saint Marx*, the passages above also show that Gorz could not guide himself, not even a little, without an enormous portion of religiosity when he addressed the possibilities of action of the *non-class of non-workers*.

at the same time that can provoke "directly a growth in human capacity", can also "sacrifice individuals in this process (and even entire classes)".[32]

The presence of the Global South in the core of the Global North through brutal social exclusion, explosive rates of structural unemployment and the elimination of various professions in the world of work – due to technological development aimed *exclusively at the creation of exchange values* – are just some of the most evident and direct examples of the social barriers that block, under capitalism, the search for a life full of meaning, endowed with an emancipated dimension for the labouring social being. It becomes apparent, however, that *alienation* is an exclusively *socio-historical* phenomenon, that in each historical moment presents itself in forms that are always diverse and, therefore, can never be conceived as a *condition humaine*, as a natural feature of the social being.[33] In Lukács' words:

> [...] alienation as a general category does not exist, even less suprahistorically, anthropologically. Alienation always has socio-historical characteristics, in each formation and each period appears *ex novo*, and is put in movement by the social forces effectively operating it.[34]

When it comes to *alienation* in the world of production – economic *alienation*, the fetishization of labour and its consciousness – a large distance is maintained between the producers and the result of their labour, the product, which confronts them as something strange, alien, as a thing. This *alienation* is also present in the labour process itself, with a higher or lower intensity. The *unidentity* between the *individual* that works and his or her dimension as a *species-being* was not eliminated also. Moreover, the diverse manifestations of *alienation*, beyond the space of production, had and even stronger impact in the *consumption* sphere. *Free time*, life *outside* work, to a great extent became *time also subjected to the values of the commodity-producing system. The labouring social being must have only what is necessary to live, but needs to be constantly induced to want to live to have or dream about new products.*

Alongside this *induction* to consume there is an enormous *reduction* of needs, in the sense that

> the most significant form of expression of the impoverishment of needs (and of capacities) is the reduction in homogenisation of needs. Both

---

32   György Lukács, *Ontologia dell'Essere Sociale II*, vol. 2 (Roma: Riuniti, 1981), 562.
33   Ibid., 559.
34   Ibid., 585.

are characteristic of the dominant classes as much as of the working class, but not in the same way [...] For the dominant classes this 'having' is effective possession [...] The worker's need to have relates instead to mere survival: he lives in order to be able to maintain himself.[35]

Hence, we are in the opposite direction of those who defend the loss of meaning of *alienation*, as a social phenomenon, when one thinks about the subjectivity of the *class-that-lives-from-labour* in contemporary society. As we tried to show previously, we believe that the ongoing changes in the labour process, despite some *epidermic* modifications, have not eliminated the basic determinations of alienation. Consequently, the actions triggered in the world of work against several expressions of alienation still have a huge relevance in the universe of contemporary sociability.

Therefore, to conclude this text, it is necessary to point out that, contrary to those formulations that envision the end of social struggles between classes, it is possible to recognize the persistence of social antagonisms between *total social capital* and the *totality of labour*, even if they assume particularities related to the various elements that characterize them: the region, country, economy, society, culture, gender, place in the international division of labour, etc. Capital's globalized character makes it necessary to also apprehend the particularities and singularities that exists in the clashes between social classes, both in capitalist advanced countries and the ones on the periphery of the system – to which a significant range of intermediate and industrialized countries belong, such as Brazil. This configures a long-term research project, this essay being only a first result, in which we tried to apprehend some of the ongoing tendencies and metamorphoses in the world of work.

---

35   Agnes Heller, *The Theory of Need in Marx* (London: Allison & Busby, 1974), 57.

PART 2

Labour's New Morphology

CHAPTER 5

The Explosion of the New Services Proletariat of the Digital Age

1   The End of the Myth[1]

Contrary to the well-known thesis about the breakdown of the law of value,[2] today's capitalism has developed into a manifold process, in which informality, precarious labour, materiality and immateriality became vital mechanisms for the preservation and amplification of the law of value. The enormous expansion of the service industry sector and of so-called immaterial labour appears to confirm this hypothesis, given their prominent role in today's digital-informational capitalism. The myth that the 'post-industrial service society' would finally cancel the proletariat and consequently the theory of value, has dissolved into thin air. Contrary to this misinterpretation, there is an emerging mass of salaried workers that is quickly expanding and providing new elements to the theory of value.

Therefore, the central hypothesis presented in this article is that the different forms of work in contemporary capitalism have neither diminished the law of value nor made it irrelevant. On the contrary, they have amplified the forms of validity of the law of value, albeit often under the appearance of non-value. This occurs due to the increasing level of invisibility of male and female workers[3] employed in the information and communication technology sectors (ICT), in call centres, in telemarketing, in the hotel industry, in cleaning companies, in commerce, in fast foods, in hypermarkets, care services, etc. by means of labour that is intermittent, part time, temporary, contractless, informal, freelance, etc.

---

1   Translated by Eugenio Mattiazzo and Rosa Bianca di Tullio, and edited by Murillo van der Laan.
2   Jürgen Habermas, "Technology and Science as 'Ideology'", in *Toward a Rational Society: Student Protest, Science, and Politics* (Boston: Beacon Press, 1989); André Gorz, *The immaterial* (London: Seagull Books, 2010); Robert Kurz, *Der Kollaps der Modernisierung: vom Zusammenbruch des Kasernen Sozialismus zur Krise der Weltokonomie* (Frankfurt am Main: Vito von Eichborn GmbH & Co. Verlag, 1991).
3   We will always use the notion of "workers" contemplating a gender dimension, as male and female workers, since an unequal and differentiated socio-sexual division clearly exists in the world of work.

As capital can accumulate value only if it creates an interaction between living and dead labour, it tries to augment the productivity of work by amplifying the mechanisms of value extraction through the expansion of dead labour, embodied in the techno-scientific-informational machinery, combined with the intensification and diversification of living labour.[4] In this process, every possible space can potentially produce surplus value. Privatized and commodified services reconfigure themselves as a new and fundamental element for understanding the new mechanisms used by capital.

An emblematic example is the zero-hour contract, a perverse form of labour that thrives in the United Kingdom, as well as elsewhere. It doesn't entail a fixed number of hours: male and female workers in the most diverse activities remain at their disposal waiting for a call. When they receive this call, they are paid only for the time they actually work and not for all the time they remained waiting. Computerised capital is increasingly making use of this method of complete flexibilization of the labour market which astutely creates a new form of digital slavery. In this way, on one side, perpetual availability for work is pushed forward, facilitated by the expansion of online work. On the other side, the plague of total precariousness spreads, robbing workers of more of their existing rights.

Uber is another emblematic example. Male and female workers using their own cars, that is to say working with their own tools, must pay all the expenses for the car's maintenance, insurance, fuel, etc. The 'app' is, in fact, a global private enterprise that uses wage work masked as 'independent' and 'entrepreneurial' work. It appropriates the surplus value generated by the services of drivers, without having to worry about worker's rights, maintenance costs, etc.

Another example of these masked forms of labour exploitation could be found in Italy, where a form of occasional and intermittent work was recently experimented, voucher-based work. Male and female workers were paid with vouchers, with values corresponding to the number of hours they have worked. Precariousness, however, was not the only problem with this form of labour, the trick was even vaster. Vouchers had to be paid at the minimum legal wage per hour, but contractors also offered extra-hours outside the voucher relation, paying an amount inferior to that of the minimum wage level. That meant achieving a level of precariousness and exploitation superior to that of

---

4 Jean Lojkine, *A Revolução Informacional* (São Paulo: Editora Cortez, 1995); Ricardo Antunes, *The Meanings of Work* (Chicago: Haymarket, 2013) and "The New Morphology of Labour and its Main Trends: Informalisation, Precarisation, (Im)materiality and Value", *Critique*, vol. 44, no. 1–2 (2016).

occasional and intermittent work. For this reason, this practice was disavowed by the Italian trade unions and the Italian Government had to suspend it.

These new forms of informal, part-time, temporary, independent, occasional or intermittent labour caused the development of a movement called precariat. This movement is quickly expanding in core capitalist countries, such as Italy, Spain, England, France, Portugal, and the United States. As it is difficult for this movement to find space inside the traditional structures of trade unions, it is developing independently at their margins.

Pioneering examples of this process can be found, for example, in Italy, with the cases of 'San Precario', in Milan, a movement fighting in defence of the precariat (including, of course, immigrants), and of the *Clash City Workers* movement, that has a strong presence in Naples and is made up of precarious workers and young people.[5] Apart from these cases, new trade union organizations have also been founded in order to represent this weaker and more precarious segment of the proletariat, some examples are the *Confederazione Unitaria di Base* (CUP) and, more recently, the NIdiL (*Nuove Identità di Lavoro*), which is part of CGIL, one of the main Italian trade union organizations.

It thus happens that, spurred by this logic, a kind of 'uberization' of labour is expanding worldwide, an entrepreneurial *modus operandi* aimed at valorising capital and generating more profit. Moreover, the fact that work is being done online has made it almost difficult to separate working time from non-working time. Permanent availability for work has thus become a reality, a kind of modern slavery in the digital age.

The foundation of these practices that are invading the world of work reveals itself. In lean production, financial capitals demand flexible labour, no pre-established working days, no clearly defined working spaces, no fixed wages, no pre-determined activities, and no labour rights – not even the right to organize in trade unions. Even the system of 'goals' is itself flexible: tomorrow's goals must always be superior to the ones of the previous day.

What should convince us that the examples we are putting forward are no longer exceptions and have become the rule? What kind of metamorphosis is

---

5 Clash City Workers is a collective of female and male unemployed workers, who define themselves as "precarious youths". In the words of the organisers of the movement: "our name means 'fighting workers of the metropolis'. Our movement was founded in mid-2009. We are particularly active in Naples, Florence, Milan and Bergamo, but we try to support all ongoing social fights throughout Italy". "Chi Siamo", Clash City Workers, Accessed 10 October 2020, http://clashcityworkers.org/chi-siamo.html. See also the study about this collective group in Clash City Workers, *Dove Sono i Nostri: Lavoro, Classe e Movimenti nell'Itália della crisi* (Lucca: La Casa Usher, 2014).

taking place in the world of services? If they were predominantly considered, in 19th and 20th centuries, as unproductive for capital, what is happening in the 21st century, in the information-digital age? Must services now be considered productive, as creators of value?

A good starting point is to recover some of Marx's indications.

2   Service Work and Marx's Fundamental Clues

In volume 2 of *Capital*, Marx offers empirical and analytical clues to understand (and update) the labour theory of value today,[6] since the productive world, broadly speaking, has expanded in new ways of generating value. Capital cannot be effective without some kind of interaction between living and dead labour. Therefore, it creates and re-creates, produces and destroys, generates new productive spaces, re-spatializes and also de-spatializes and is always intimately linked to the generation of value.

In the machine-informational-digital world which developed intensively in recent decades, the production time has decreased and the spaces that generate value were extended. If the surplus value is born in the production sphere,[7] we know that capital's cycle also includes distribution, circulation and consumption. In volume 2, Marx comprehensively addressed the process of capital circulation[8] and in volume 3 he analysed the process of capitalist production as a whole.[9]

As the main objective of capital is its valorisation, the reduction of circulation time becomes imperative. In addition, as the total time of capital depends on both production time and circulation time, one of the daily challenges of the engineering of capital is to decrease the difference in its overall time. According to Marx:

> the duration of its sojourn in the sphere of production is its time of production, that of its stay in the sphere of circulation its time of circulation

---

6   Karl Marx, "Capital. Volume 2: The Process of Circulation of Capital", in *Karl Marx & Friedrich Engels, Collected Works, vol. 36* (London: Lawrence & Wishart, 1997).
7   Karl Marx, "Capital. Volume 1: The Process of Production of Capital", in *Karl Marx & Friedrich Engels, Collected Works, vol. 35* (London: Lawrence & Wishart, 1996).
8   Marx, "Capital. Volume 2".
9   Karl Marx, "Capital. Volume 3: *The Process of Capitalist Production as a Whole*", in *Karl Marx & Friedrich Engels, Collected Works, vol. 37* (London: Lawrence & Wishart, 1998).

or rotation. The total time during which it describes its circuit is therefore equal to the sum of its time of production and its time of circulation.[10]

Thus, while commodities are not traded, the surplus value created in production is not realized. Therefore, circulation time, although necessary, becomes a limit to production time. In this way, its reduction is always urgent in order to shorten the total turnover time of capital.

Therefore, the more capital circulation time approaches zero, the higher is its productivity. As Marx says

> the more the metamorphoses of circulation of a certain capital are only ideal, i.e., the more the time of circulation is equal to zero, or approaches zero, the more does capital function, the more does its productivity and the self-expansion of its value increase [...] A capital's time of circulation therefore limits, generally speaking, its time of production and hence its process of generating surplus value.[11]

This is precisely why Marx indicates that, in particular situations, such as in transport, storage and communications industries, though there is not an increase in the amount of material goods produced, there is, in any case, value creation.

Marx firmly stated that

> however, what the transportation industry sells is change of location. The useful effect is inseparably connected with the process of transportation, i.e., the productive process of the transport industry. Men and goods travel together with the means of transportation, and this travelling, this locomotion, constitutes the process of production effected by these means. The useful effect can be consumed only during this process of production. It does not exist as a utility different from this process, a use thing which does not function as an article of commerce, does not circulate as a commodity, until after it has been produced. But the exchange value of this useful effect is determined, like that of any other commodity, by the value of the elements of production (labour power and means of production) consumed in it plus the surplus value created by the surplus labour of the labourers employed in transportation.[12]

---

10   Marx, "Capital. Volume 2", 125.
11   Ibid., 129.
12   Ibid., 62.

We have here a fundamental analytical clue to understand the importance that the service sector has today for capitalist accumulation. Value can be created, although, as in the case of the transport industry, there is no increase in the quantity of what is produced.[13]

Marx adds

> the productive capital invested in this industry imparts value to the transported products, partly by transferring value from the means of transportation, partly by adding value through the labour performed in transport. This last-named increment of value splits, as it does in all capitalist production, into a replacement of wages and into surplus value.[14]

This leads him to conclude that

> the transport industry forms on the one hand an independent branch of production and thus a separate sphere of investment of productive capital. On the other hand, its distinguishing feature is that it appears as a continuation of a process of production *within* the process of circulation and *for* the process of circulation.[15]

Thus, for Marx, activity in the transport industry can be described as a "productive process inside the process of circulation". This formulation provides an important analytical clue for understanding the capitalist world of services as producing value, because it shows us a productive process at work inside the transport industry. Since Marx has an amplified notion of industry,[16] it becomes possible to understand why there is a 'process of production' in the transport sector (and in other sectors, such as storage, gas industry, railways, seafaring, communication, etc.), even if this activity does not result in any material production.

In this sense, the transport industry, an expression of an immaterial form of production that takes place in the sphere of circulation, is not only indispensable for the creation of surplus value in other industries, but it also incorporates a 'process of production' in itself, even if it does not produce anything material and touchable.

---

13   Ibid., 153.
14   Ibid., 153–154.
15   Ibid., 155.
16   Ibid., 155.

We know that these examples, taken from the sphere of circulation do not mean that surplus value is always created outside production. The latter is, in fact, its vital space. Marx, however, demonstrates that the sphere of production covers a wider space than mere material production. This does not mean that all processes that generate profit also generate surplus value. We can recall, as an example, that when Marx deals with commerce, in volume 3, he says that even if trade is an essential activity, it does not generate surplus value and for this reason, commerce must be considered unproductive.[17]

Marx adds that commercial capital appropriates part of the surplus value created in industrial production and therefore is not responsible for its production. He also points out, however, that the condition of commerce workers is very similar to that of other workers.

First, they receive a wage just like any other worker. In other words, the commercial bourgeoisie purchases them with variable capital and not with rent.[18] Second, the value of the labour power of male and female commerce workers is determined by the costs of production and reproduction of labour power, just as it is for the whole of the working class . Marx, however, adds that there is a fundamental difference between industrial workers and commerce workers, the same difference that can be found between industrial and commercial capitalists. While industrial proletariat generates surplus value, wageworkers employed in commerce do not.[19]

Thus, if it is clear that for Marx commerce has not developed as a productive activity, the same cannot be said of his analysis of certain services in Volume 2 of Capital and both in Chapter 19 of volume 1 and in the unpublished Chapter 6, *Results of the Direct Production Process*, where Marx provides the examples of teachers, writers, singers, among others.[20]

More than 150 years after these fundamental clues were written, many radical changes have taken place in the capitalism of the digital-informational and financial age. It is now imperative to update our understanding about the way work in services contributes (or does not contribute) to the creation of exchange value and surplus value. As we have already anticipated, our hypothesis is that we are witnessing new forms of extraction of surplus value in the spheres of non-material or immaterial production, especially in those parts of the service sector that have been privatized and commodified. We should

---

17 See Marx, "Capital. Volume 3", especially chapter 17 "The Commercial Profit", 279–300.
18 Ibid., 291–292.
19 Ibid., 299.
20 See Marx, "Capital. Volume 1"; "Chapter Six. Results of the Direct Production Process", *in Karl Marx & Friedrich Engels, Collected Works, vol. 34*. (London: Lawrence & Wishart, 1994).

keep in mind that the main transformation of the flexible enterprise was not due to science becoming the main productive force,[21] but to the progressive imbrication of work and science, materiality and immateriality, productive and unproductive labour.[22]

Now, the most important social and political consequence of this amplification of the theory of value is the growth of who Ursula Huws suggestively called cybertariat[23] and Ruy Braga and myself called infoproletariat.[24]

This amplification of service activities in the process of capital valorisation takes us to another related topic. In the universe of immaterial production – information and communication technologies, call centres, telemarketing, etc. – can we affirm that work can also generate value and, therefore, becomes productive?

3 Can Immaterial Labour Generate Surplus Value?

In order to answer this question, we now need to introduce two definitions that are central to our argument. The first one is the distinction between materiality and immateriality of production and labour.

We owe Marx the distinction between material and immaterial production.[25] He states that in order to be productive, it is no longer necessary to work manually, but to be part of an organ belonging to the whole of productive labour, performing any one of its functions. Marx adds that the predominance of material production is valid in the case of collective production understood as a whole, but it is no longer valid for labour considered in isolation.[26]

He also claims that only the worker who produces surplus value for the capitalist is productive – that is to say, if the worker takes part in the process of capital valorisation. After referring to the example of the teacher, whose activity Marx considers to be external to the sphere of material production, he says

---

21   Habermas, "Technology and Science as 'Ideology'"; "The New Obscurity", in *The New Conservatism: Cultural Criticism and the Historians' Debate* (Cambridge: Polity Press, 1989).
22   Antunes, *The Meanings of Work.*; István Mészáros, *The Power of Ideology* (London: Harvester Wheatsheaf, 1989).
23   Ursula Huws, *The Making of a Cybertariat: virtual work in a real world* (New York: Monthly Review Press, 2003).
24   Ricardo Antunes & Ruy Braga (ed.), *Infoproletários: Degradação Real do Trabalho Virtual* (São Paulo: Boitempo, 2009).
25   Here we should return to Marx's indication in "Capital. Volume 1", especially chapter 14; and in "Chapter Six. Results of the Direct Production Process".
26   See Marx, "Capital. Volume 1", 509–510.

that a teacher is productive when he is under the command of a capitalist who owns a "teaching factory". However, the same teacher is unproductive when his teaching produces only use-value and not exchange value. Productive labour occurs only within a social relationship that is predominantly aimed at the self-valorisation of capital.[27]

We want to highlight the fact that Marx acknowledges the existence of activities, not predominantly material, in the valorisation of capital. However, as we have seen, he adds that material production remains the dominant form of production in capitalism. For this reason, it is important to emphasize that the myth about an immaterial production not based on materiality is an Eurocentric (or Northern) creation that has no real ontological basis, not in capitalist core countries and even less if we consider global production as a whole, including China, India, Brazil, Mexico, Korea and South Africa, among others.[28]

The second central point concerns the conceptualization of productive and unproductive labour. We shall summarize this distinction in six main points, extracting them from our synthesis of Marx's work. Productive labour is the labour that:

1) creates surplus value and valorises capital;
2) is paid by means of capital-money and not in the form of rent. Rent is, on the contrary, the form of payment that characterizes unproductive labour, which produces use-value but does not produce exchange-value;
3) is the result of collective, social and complex forms of labour, as opposed to individual labour. For this reason, Marx says that it is not the individual worker who is the real agent of the labour process as a whole, but rather a socially combined labour capacity;
4) valorises capital, independent of the fact that its products are material or immaterial;
5) depends on the social relation and social form within which capital is created and valorised. Precisely for this reason, work activities that are identical in their tangible nature, may be productive or unproductive depending on their relation to the creation of value;
6) tends to be salaried, even if the inverse is not true, because not all salaried work is productive.

---

27 Ibid., 510.
28 Antunes, *The Meanings of Work*.

On the other hand, labour is unproductive when it only creates useful goods and it is not involved in the production of exchange value. For this reason, capitalism tries to eliminate all unnecessary unproductive labour, besides merging productive and unproductive activities, whenever it is possible.

If this is Marx's formulation for describing capitalism in the mid-19th century, today we are witnessing the rise of new forms of validity and amplification of the law of value, which are capable of creating complex mechanisms for surplus value extraction, both in the material and immaterial spheres that characterize the expanding global chains of value in contemporary capitalism. Instead of weakening the law of value, this conjunction has amplified it, making it more complex and ultimately has intensified its effects in the 21st century.[29]

This is because immaterial labour has come to play a relevant, though not dominant, role in value formation, not only because it is part of the relational articulation between different forms of living labour interacting with dead labour, but also because it influences the process of valorisation of capital by reducing capital circulation time and consequently also capital rotation time. This is especially true for the service sectors (and for their intersections, as for example the agribusiness industry, the service industry and the industrial services) that are being increasingly controlled by the logic of capital and its commodification process. This sector is being gradually integrated in the chains of value production and so it is abandoning its unproductive form by becoming increasingly part of the process of value creation.

The main criticism to the thesis of the validity of the theory of value in immaterial production is that this type of labour is intangible.[30] Today's capitalism appears to have cancelled this objection, since value depends increasingly on forms of labour that are collective and social, complex and aggregated.[31] In the new productive chains material and immaterial labour are imbricated and interrelated. Consequently, immaterial labour has become an essential and vital component of the commodity-form.[32]

---

29   Huws, *The Making of a Cybertariat*; Antunes, *The Meanings of Work*; Vinícius Santos, *Trabalho Imaterial e Teoria do Valor em Marx* (São Paulo: Expressão Popular, 2013).
30   André Gorz, *The immaterial*.
31   It is worth remembering that Toyota had painted the following words at the entrance of its factory in Takaoda: "*Yoi kangae, yoi shina*" (good thoughts equal good products). The Japanese industry could appreciate the value of an information while critics of the theory of value were denying it. (*Business Week*, 18/11/2003).
32   André Tosel, "Centralité et Non-Centralité du Travail ou La Passion des Hommes Superflus", in *La Crise du Travail. Actuel Marx Confrontation*, ed. Jacques Bidet & Jacques Texier (Paris: Presses Universitaries de France, 1995); Antunes, *The Meanings of Work*.

An emblematic example of this extension of the law of value to areas that were previously considered unproductive can be seen in the global diffusion of outsourcing in all the branches of production and particularly in the service sector. Following our conception, outsourcing is one of the main mechanisms used by capitalism in order to intensify the extraction of surplus value – expanding the incidence of value from industry and agriculture to services, thus extending the possibility of capital valorisation to a sector that, in the past, was considered less important by capitalism. The global expansion of outsourcing companies that offer 'industrial services' is exemplary.[33]

Now, if the hypothesis presented here is valid, its social and political effects should also be evident and of great relevance. The nature of these effects could be summarized in the following questions: should male and female workers in the service sector be considered an emerging middle class? Or should they be considered part of a precariat, what we called a new services proletariat? This is what we will discuss in the last section of this article.

4   Middle Class, Precariat or the New Service Proletariat?

The male and female workers of the service sector (call centres, telemarketing, software and information and communication technologies industries, hotels, shopping centres, hypermarkets, fast-foods, large-scale retailers, among many others), are becoming increasingly separated from the forms of intellectual work that are typical of the middle class and are coming closer to what we call the new services proletariat.

If the more traditional segments of the middle class are defined by the modalities of their participation in production, with predominantly intellectual and non-manual (doctors, lawyers and the other liberal professions) activities, then currently there is an expansion of intermediate layers of wageworkers.

---

[33] Foxconn, for example, is an industry that produces parts for information and communication technologies products. It provides an excellent example of the 'Electronic Contract Manufacturing', as a global outsourcing enterprise that is responsible for assembling electronic products for Nokia, Apple and many other multinational corporations. In its factory in Longhua (Shenzen), where iPhones are assembled, there has been a long series of suicides of male and female workers, the majority of cases probably motivated by the intense exploitation of labour to which female and male workers were submitted. See Pun Ngai & Jenny Chan, *The Advent of Capital Expansion in China: A Case Study of Foxconn Production and the Impacts on its Workers*, Accessed 10 October 2020, http://rdln.files.wordpress.com/2012/01/pun-ngai_chan-jenny_on-foxconn.pdf. See also Antunes, *The Meanings of Work*.

Made up of bank clerks, teachers, workers in commerce, in supermarkets, in fast food, in call-centres, in information and technology firms, etc., this layer is going through an increasing process of proletarianization, reinforcing Braverman's pioneering formulation.[34]

Due to their typical structural fluctuations, the middle classes are also defined by their ideals and their cultural, symbolic and consumption values.[35] The higher segments of the middle classes separate themselves from the lower ones and position themselves, in the valuation sphere, closer to the proprietary classes. On the other hand, in their lowest strata, the salaried middle class tends to be closer, in an objective dimension, to the working classes.

This is why middle-class consciousness often appears as the consciousness of a non-class. In some cases, they are closer to proprietary classes, such as middle and upper management, executives, engineers, doctors, lawyers; but in other cases, when we consider the poorer segments of the middle classes, they are under living and working conditions very similar to those of the working class.

These more proletarianized contingents, especially those who are employed in the service sector, are increasingly involved (directly or indirectly) in the process of capital valorisation. Wageworkers at call centres, telemarketing, fast-food workers, large-scale retailers, offices, hotels, restaurants find themselves extremely close to this new proletariat, which is expanding globally and is the current protagonist of many social struggles, rallies and strikes worldwide.

Therefore, we disagree not only with analysts that classify these sectors as middle class, but also with authors who think that they are part of an alleged 'new class', the 'precariat class'.[36]

Our previous studies have emphasized that since the emergence of capital's structural crisis[37] the structural precariousness of labour is expanding significantly. The intensification of labour exploitation, which is increasingly becoming a super-exploitation of the labour power, has caused an enormous rise in the levels of informality, outsourcing and precariousness – a process that occurs not only in the Global South, but also in Northern countries.[38]

---

34 Harry Braverman, *Labor and Monopoly Capital* (New York: Monthly Review Press, 1974).
35 Pierre Bordieu, *Distinction: A social critique of the judgement of taste* (Cambridge: Harvard University Press, 2002).
36 Guy Standing, *The Precariat: The New Dangerous Class* (London: Bloomsbury, 2011).
37 István Mészáros, *Beyond Capital: Towards a Theory of Transition* (London: Merlin Press, 1995); Robert Kurz, *Der Kollaps der Modernisierung*; François Chesnais, *A Mundialização do Capital* (São Paulo: Editora Xamã, 1996).
38 Ricardo Antunes, "The New Morphology of the Working Class in Contemporary Brazil", in *Socialist Register 2015: Transforming Classes*, ed. Leo Panitch and Greg Albo (London: Merlin Press, 2014).

It was in this context that the social landscape changed substantively. In Portugal, for instance, social struggles became emblematic: the unrest of *Geração à Rasca* exploded in March 2011. Thousands of demonstrators, young people and immigrants, precarious and unemployed women and men gave expression to their revolt in the *Precari@s inflexíveis* movement.

In Spain, the movement of 'indignados' started with young people protesting against the high levels of unemployment and the complete lack of life perspectives: studying or not studying they were doomed to be unemployed or, at best, to have precarious jobs.

In England, a vast social uprising exploded after a black taxi driver was killed by police. In a few days, the revolt of poor, black, immigrant and unemployed youths spread to many cities. This was the first significant social uprising in England (and in parts of the United Kingdom), since the protests against the Poll Tax that put an end to Margaret Thatcher's government.

In the United States, the mass movement *Occupy Wall Street* rose to denounce the hegemonic interests of financial capital and its nefarious social consequences: the increase in unemployment rates and the epidemic of precarious labour, which hit women, blacks and immigrants harder.

Finally, we have already mentioned the emergence, in Italy, of new social movements representing the precariat. The 2001 *MayDay* uprising, in Milan, gave birth to a movement that struggles for rights and for an independent representation of this heterogeneous mass of skilled and unskilled workers, young people and immigrants (San Precario).[39]

All these cases, and many others, spurred a debate about the rise of this new contingent of the working class. In this debate, Guy Standing presented the most polemical perspective, claiming that a 'new class' was emerging: the precariat.[40]

According to Standing, the precariat must be considered a separate class, different from the one formed in industrial capitalism, during the Taylorist-Fordist period. In this view, the precariat is closer to a new and more disorganized class, ideologically dispersed and easily attracted to 'populist policies', susceptible even to 'neo-fascist' calls. Despite the fact that the description Standing gives of the precariat contains, indeed, some relevant information, he characterizes this new class as a 'dangerous class', distinct in-itself and for-itself from the working class.[41]

---

39 "Chi Siamo", San Precario, Accessed 10 October, 2020, https://www.precaria.org/info. Above we also mentioned the Italian group *Clash City Workers*.
40 Standing, *The Precariat*.
41 Ibid., 1–25; see also *Global Labour Journal*, vol. 7, n. 2 (2016), Special Issue (May): *Politics of Precarity – Critical Engagements with Guy Standing*.

Our formulation goes in the opposite direction of those that describes the precariat as a new class. We believe that the new morphology of the class-that-lives-from-labour encompasses distinct segments, even if they may present themselves in very different ways. Difference is not new in the history of the working class and was always present in gender, age, ethnicity, nationality, migration, skills, etc.

Therefore, instead of being a separate class, we consider the precariat as a distinct sector of the working class, in all its heterogeneity, differentiation and fragmentation. In advanced capitalist countries, the more precarious individuals – either young, immigrant, black, etc. – are already born under the weight of the corrosion of rights, and struggle in every possible way to win them back.

On the other hand, the more traditional sectors of the working class, heirs of the welfare state, struggle to stop an even greater collapse of their working conditions. The future of these two fundamental poles of the same class-that-lives-from-labour appears inextricably linked. The precarious young people, in their struggles, dream of a better world and want to put an end to the complete precariousness that suffocates their lives. The traditional workers, better represented both in trade unions and politics, want to avoid an even greater degradation of their working conditions and refuse their conversion into precarious workers.

Capital's destructive logic has multiple ways of manifesting itself, but in its essence is one. For this reason, if these two vital poles of the world of work were not capable of joining in a solidary and organic way, they will suffer an even greater defeat.

Precariousness is a trend that arises, as Marx demonstrated in *Capital*, with the very creation of wage labour in capitalism.[42] As the working class sells its labour power and only receives a part of its production, the surplus that is produced and appropriated by capital tends to expand through various mechanisms intrinsic to capitalism.

As capitals often seek to increase surplus value (both relative and absolute), the expansion of the unequal exchange between the value that the proletariat produces and what it receives is an inherent trend in the very logic of capitalism. Various mechanisms are used to achieve this goal, such as the intensification of labour, extension of the working hours, restriction and limitation of rights etc. Since it is the result of this class struggle, the precariousness of the working class is a process that can be increased or reduced, due to the

---

42 Ricardo Antunes, "The New Service Proletariat", *Monthly Review*, vol. 69 (2018), 1–7.

intensification of the capitalist exploitation or the working class capacity to resist through strikes and trade union struggles.

This is why both Marx and Engels have demonstrated that the forms of exploitation of labour are incessantly alternated, phenomena that are accentuated by the expansion of the relative surplus population, which allows capital to use surplus labour in order to intensify and increase the levels of exploitation and consequent precariousness of the working class more and more.

In current capitalism, the relative surplus population, which Marx, in *Capital* has designated as floating, latent, stagnant, acquires new dimensions.[43] This occurs through the enormous expansion and circulation of immigrant labour power on a global scale, increasing even more the mechanisms of exploitation, intensification and precariousness of labour power. The destruction of hard-won social rights becomes an imposition of capital's global system in its phase of financial hegemony.

As a consequence, we have a heterogeneous working class, differentiated also by branches, sectors and the international division of labour, especially the division between North and South. If Engels had already demonstrated, in his excellent work *The Condition of the Working Class in England*, that the British working class was very heterogeneous and differentiated, these cleavages are accentuated when one perceives the differential rate of exploitation practiced between centre and periphery.

The outcome of these processes depends on the ability of the working class to resist, organize and fight back. If the two poles of the working class manage to establish solidarity links and a sense of class belonging[44] and if they are united in their everyday fights, they will be able to create a stronger and better organized opposition to the logic of capital, which is profoundly averse to labour.

In this respect, the role of the new service proletariat is emblematic. Its integration as a constitutive and growing part of an expanded working class, its participation in the clashes and resistances will be decisive for the outcome of the struggles of the working class as a whole.

Finally, given the uneven and combined nature of the international division of labour it is necessary to draw some mediations in order to define the precariat. The first concerns the cleavage between the Global North and South. In the periphery of capitalism, the proletariat was born under the weight of precariousness. It suffices to say that in Brazil and in many other countries in

---

43 See Marx, "Capital. Volume 1", chapter 23.
44 Alain Bihr, *Du 'Grand Soir' a 'L'Alternative': Le Mouvement Ouvrier Européen en Crise* (Paris: Les Editions Ouvrieres, 1991).

Latin America (not to mention USA), the proletariat emerged directly from the abolition of slave labour. Consequently, precariousness has never been an exception, but a constant characteristic of the proletariat in these countries.

Since countries in the Global South never developed an enduring labour aristocracy, the proletariat has always been associated with a condition of precariousness; its internal differences were never as evident as they are in the North. Here, on the contrary, a labour aristocracy historically developed first and later came the proletariat inheritor of the welfare state. The recent emergence of the precariat has generated an expressive differentiation in the working class of the North that has no parallel in the South. In the periphery of capitalism, the internal cleavages of the working class are not as intense as they are in core countries. In this sense, to conceptualize a 'new class' becomes an even greater mistake.

Therefore, if seems reasonable to empirically identify the recent emergence of the precariat as one of the poles of the working class in core countries, in the periphery of capitalism something different takes place. This is due to the fact that in the Global South the precariat has constituted the working class since its origins, even if nowadays it may be assuming new articulations. Either under the name of precariat, or as part of the new service proletariat, these are female and male workers who are heterogeneous in their forms of being (gender, ethnicity, skills, nationality, etc.) and homogeneous with respect to their precarious condition, deprived of rights and contractual guarantees.

The forms of intensification of work: the disregard for rights; super-exploitation; the condition of living between formality and informality; the pressure of goals; despotism of bosses, coordinators and supervisors; degraded salaries; the intermittent labour; harassments; illnesses and deaths, all point to a strong process of proletarianization and to the explosion of a new service proletariat that is expanding worldwide, diversifying and amplifying the working class.

Moreover, if there is a new morphology of labour, we should at the same time acknowledge the emergence of a new morphology of working-class forms of organization, representation and struggle. The current world has been an extraordinary laboratory for understanding this new era of social struggle.

CHAPTER 6

Freeze-Dried Flexibility

A New Morphology of Labour: Casualisation and Value

1   Introduction[1]

The 20th century can be briefly characterised as the century of the automobile. The structure of production was developed through the binomial Taylorist-Fordist system: a factory (extending towards society) producing goods under the strict control of capital. Taylor said that workers should perform their prescribed work under strict control over time and motion and that there should be a layer of managers responsible for the development and control of production.[2]

This produced a timed and homogeneous output with a controlled pace, aiming for a situation where, as Ford reputedly said, the consumer's options amounted to choosing between one T-Model black Ford car and another T-Model black Ford car. Conceived in a serial, rigid and piecemeal rhythm, the assembly line generated mass production that aimed to increase mass consumption in a situation where workers' wages were also increased.

This productive materiality spread to the world of industry and services (even McDonalds can be regarded as stemming from these origins) and can be seen as represented symbolically in Chaplin's brilliant film, *Modern Times*: the degradation of unilateral, standardised, piecemeal, fetishized, objectified, mechanical, massified labour, with even workers' sexuality controlled through Taylorism and Fordism. Although regulated and contracted, the degradation of labour in this society was characterised by its mechanisation, fragmentation, manualisation, alienation and, ultimately, dehumanisation. This situation was dominant until the early 1970s, when a structural crisis of the productive system occurred that can be regarded as somehow extended to the present day, since the vast and global productive restructuring process has not yet completed its cycle. But it appeared then that the venture based on Taylorism and Fordism had completed its trajectory. It was then a matter of implementing

---

1   This was first published in *Work Organisation, Labour & Globalisation*, vol. 5, no.1 (2011). Translated by Jean Pierre Barakat and edited by Ursula Huws.
2   Frederick Winslow Taylor, *Principles of Scientific Management* (New York and London: Harper & Brothers, 1911).

new accumulation mechanisms and forms that could offer answers to the critical situation that was unfolding, especially after the outbreak of social struggles of 1968 in France or Italy's 'Hot Autumn' in 1969, whose movements aimed at the social control of production.

There were several experiments exercised by capital in its restructuring process: in Sweden (Kalmar), in northern Italy, in the so-called 'Third Italy', in California, in the USA, in the UK, in Germany and in several other countries and regions, with the Japanese Toyota experiment being the most significant, since it had been developing its structure since the early 1950s and showed strong universalising potential after the 1973 crisis years. For capital, the goal was to ensure accumulation, but in an increasingly flexible way, compatible with the new phase of capital development. The so-called flexible company could be said to have been born then.

This structural change was strengthened after the victories of neoliberalism, when a new recipe, or ideo-political design, appeared as an alternative dominant form, replacing that of the welfare state. An alternative practice began to spread which was closely articulated with the ongoing restructuring of production on a global scale. A new form of engineering, which could be named 'freeze-drying' was structured into the production process. This restructuring process was based on a dominant ideology variously known as 'lean production', or the 'lean enterprise', or 'modern enterprise' – a form of enterprise that restricts and limits living labour (i.e., human labour) by extending the techno-scientific machinery, which Marx called 'dead labour'. It redesigned the production plant quite differently from Taylorism/Fordism, by greatly reducing the living workforce and intensively increasing its productivity, reterritorializing and sometimes even de-territorializing the world of production, in a process in which the notions of space and time were profoundly transformed.

The result was quick to emerge: an explosive growth in unemployment, structural instability of labour, lowering of wages and loss of workers' rights. An expansion occurred, which Juan Castillo inspirationally named 'organisational lyophilisation' (or 'freeze-drying'): a process whereby living substances are removed and living labour is increasingly replaced by dead labour.[3] A new kind of labour was required in this 'freeze-dried' company, a kind of labour which is mystified by employers by such usages as the one in which workers are termed 'collaborators' or 'partners'. What are the contours of this new kind of labour?

---

3 Juan Castillo, "Sociologia del Trabajo", in *Colección 'Monografías' 152* (Madrid: Centro de Investigaciones Sociológicas, 1996).

Above all, it should be more 'versatile' and 'multifunctional' than the labour that developed under the Taylorist and Fordist company. The form of labour that is increasingly being sought by companies is not one based on Taylorist and Fordist specialisation, but a form that flourished during the stage of 'multifunctional de-specialisation', or 'multifunctional labour', a concept which encapsulates the enormous intensification that has occurred in the rhythms, timing and processes of labour. This has occurred both in industrial work and in services, as well as in agribusiness, dissolving the traditional divisions between agriculture, manufacturing and services.

The results seem obvious: an intensification of the ways in which labour is extracted, an expansion of outsourcing, and a metamorphosis of the notions of time and space. Cumulatively, this introduces considerable changes in the way that capital produces goods, whether these are tangible or immaterial, corporeal or symbolic. Several smaller units interconnected by a network can replace a single concentrated business, with a much lower number of workers and producing many times more. Telematic work, network-connected work and new forms of homeworking emerge with distinctive forms of instability. These impact on labour in its organisational, evaluative, subjective and ideo-political dimensions. Stable forms of labour thus become almost non-existent, as we experience the erosion of the contracted and regulated types of labour that were dominant in the 20th century. These are being replaced by outsourced and flexible labour, new ways of working part time, 'entrepreneurship', 'cooperativism', 'voluntary work', 'third sector', and a range of other examples of what used to be called 'atypical work'.[4]

The example of cooperatives in Brazil is particularly poignant. Originally, cooperatives were born as a tool in workers' struggles against unemployment and labour market despotism. Now, however, employers are creating false cooperatives as a way of weakening labour rights even more. Thus, the 'cooperatives' created by companies mean something quite different from the original intention underlying the design of workers cooperatives: they have become another expression of employers' endeavours to destroy the rights and further increase the precarious conditions of the working class . A similar case is that of entrepreneurship, which is increasingly being shaped as a disguised form of waged labour, one which allows, in the scenario opened up by neoliberalism and the restructuring of production, for a proliferation of new forms of flexibilization of wages, hours, and functional or organisational structures.

---

4   Luciano Vasapollo, *O Trabalho Atípico e a Precariedade* (São Paulo: Expressão Popular, 2005).

It can now be said that we have a situation of structural labour instability in which global capital is demanding from national governments the dismantling of the protective social legislation of labour. This flexibilization of the social legislation of labour brings a further enhancement of the extraction mechanisms of overwork and expansion of the forms of instability as well as the destruction of social rights that were hard-won by the working class in the past, especially, in the Brazilian case, in the post-1930 period. This is occurring in an age of techno-scientific advancement that has seen the collapse of many (unfounded) optimistic hopes. Scientific progress, it seems, does not go hand in hand with social progress: informality is increasing in parallel with the advance of information literacy.

If we turn our gaze to the contemporary (un)sociability of the world of globalised and financialised capital, another contradiction becomes evident: the more intensively knowledge-based and communications-based the so-called 'modern enterprise' appears to be, the more streamlined is its *modus operandi,* and the more companies operate on the basis that they are deploying high levels of 'competence', 'qualifications', 'knowledge management' and 'goal-oriented' systems, the more intense are the levels of degradation of labour (in the sense of loss of ties and corrosion of regulation and hiring mechanisms) for a large and growing proportion of male and female workers.

The social pyramid of labour is further segmented in its structure: at the top are the ultra-qualified workers operating within the information arena of the so-called information and communication technologies; at the bottom, there is instability and unemployment, which are both structural, resulting from a huge labour power surplus, too large to be absorbed by capital. In the middle is hybridity, the space *par excellence* of those workers who were previously in skilled jobs but are now out of work because of the closures, transfers or mergers of the companies they previously worked for, and, especially in times of crisis, are candidates for becoming part of an undifferentiated mass of unemployed people, merging with those working men and women who have been out of work for years and are unable to return to the labour market.

There is, however, another important element in the new setting of the working world, worthy of particular mention here: this is the expansion of 'cognitive', 'intellectual', or 'immaterial' labour (labour which does not create anything objective and corporeal), performed in the spheres of communication, information, advertising and marketing, that are characteristic of a society dominated by logos, brands, the symbolic, the associative, the superfluous and the informational. That is what business discourse calls the 'knowledge society', which is present in, for instance, the designs of Microsoft software, Benetton models, or mobile phones and which stems from an immaterial labour which, articulated and inserted into tangible labour (that which creates something objective and corporeal), expresses contemporary forms of value.

By appropriating the cognitive dimension of labour and by taking possession of its intellectual dimension – a crucial feature of modern capitalism – employers expand value-generating methods and mechanisms and also increase the ways by which labour subjects can be controlled and subordinated, through the use of "more coercive mechanisms, thus renewing primitive forms of violence, since, at the same time, companies increasingly need the cooperation or the subjective and social 'involvement' of the worker".[5]

There is therefore a qualitative change and an increase in the forms and mechanisms of labour extraction, stemming from the end or reduction of the apparent relevance of the labour theory of value. The slogan adopted by Toyota at the Takaoka unit, *'Yoi kangae, yoi shina'* ('good thoughts mean good products') set on the flag hanging at the entrance of its production plants, is an illustration of this approach.

Another example is provided by Telefónica's recent project, *District C*, in Madrid, Spain, where a significant proportion of information and communication technology workers already work without a desk or workbench, circulating 'freely' throughout the company's premises, working under a system of targets. We could also instance the countless call-centre and telemarketing companies that are expanding in virtually all parts of the world and becoming increasingly important for achieving the aggregation of value.

The prevalence of instrumental reason thus takes the form of a huge societal irrationality, which creates an intense contradiction and poses a strong challenge: in order for humanity, and therefore also labour, to be truly endowed with meaning, and for the dehumanising and destructive process that has been ongoing since the industrial revolution to be brought to an end, this notion and its accompanying worldview have to be deconstructed.

The central contradiction is this: the age of computerisation of labour and of a mechanical and digital world, is also the age of labour informality, of outsourced, precarious, subcontracted, temporary and part-time work, in other words, an age of the subproletariat, .

A pendulum motion is being experienced by the working-class: on the one hand, fewer men and women work harder at a pace and intensity that resemble the bygone phases of capitalism, thus bringing about a reduction in the stability of labour inherited from the industrial stage which characterised much

---

5   Alberto Bialakowsky et al., "Dilución y Mutación del Trabajo en la Dominación Social Local", *Revista Herramienta,* no. 23 (2003), 135.

of 20th century capitalism. However, since employers cannot completely eliminate living labour, they manage to reduce it in many areas and expand it in others, as can be seen, at the same time, by the increasing appropriation of the cognitive dimension of labour and, in parallel, by the growth of unqualified and precarious labour. Here we see the signs of the perennial nature of labour. On the other side of the pendulum, though, increasingly, more men and women are finding less work and spreading across the world in search of any job they can find, thus setting a trend of increasing labour precariousness and casualisation on a global scale, from the USA to Japan, from Germany to India, and from Britain to Mexico. The expansion of structural unemployment is the most virulent manifestation of this tendency.

2   Brazil in the New International Division of Labour

When considering productive restructuring in Brazil, we can say that its first impulses occurred during the 1980s, causing companies to adopt, initially in a restricted manner, new organisational and technological patterns as well as new forms of social organisation of labour. During this period, Brazil saw the first use of productive computerisation; the use of the just in time (JIT) system was initiated; the first productive centres based on teamwork blossomed in the context of 'total quality' programs; and, in a still preliminary way, the implementation of 'participatory' methods. The, still largely dominant, Fordist model began to open up to the first influx of Toyotism and flexible accumulation.

It was in the 1990s, however, that the productive restructuring of capital developed strongly in Brazil, with the intensification of lean production, JIT systems *kanban*, total quality processes, new forms of subcontracting and outsourcing of the workforce and the transfer of production plants and units.

Both through these types of programs and through the introduction of wage deals linked to profitability and productivity (as exemplified by 'Participation in Profit Sharing and Results' – PLR – Programmes), the productive world finally created the preconditions for unleashing vigorous restructuring, including corporate downsizing and the implementation of mechanisms allowing organisations to be structured in a more flexible way. New managerial policies included the introduction of variable pay with wages linked to meeting productivity targets.

As a consequence, there was an expansion of flexible hiring practices and a significant expansion in outsourcing, for example of call-centre work, often associated with a growth in the techno-informational content of work. This increased the deregulation of labour and the reduction of workers' social rights.

Organisations were thus increasingly able to draw on 'freeze-dried' external sources of labour in an *ad hoc* manner, with an accompanying increase in the mechanisms for the individualisation of labour and wage relations.[6]

At the same time, there was a deterioration in health in the workplace and an unprecedented increase in Repetitive Strain Injury (RSI) which reduces muscle strength and compromises the movements of sufferers, manifesting itself as a typical disease of the age of labour computerisation. In a new workplace rhetoric, workers were forced to become 'partners' or 'collaborators', identities that cloud their condition as workers. Meanwhile, the increasingly intensive use of technology, new ways of organising production and the broader introduction of outsourcing led to high levels of unemployment and underemployment in many sectors, only partially offset by the growth of small businesses.

Some of the new trends in work that arose during this period included the expansion of homeworking, a growth in so-called 'labour cooperatives' and a general increase in subcontracting. These contributed to the casualisation of the workforce, increased precariousness, significant cuts in real wages and growing noncompliance with labour rights. Labour outsourcing and the return to bygone practices like the 'putting out system' expanded enormously in the textile and garment sectors, again leading to an ever-greater precariousness and casualisation of labour and breaches of labour rights.

It can be concluded that, on the one hand, Taylorist and Fordist patterns that had existed since the 1930s in Brazil were increasingly mixed with new production processes, in a cocktail of mechanisms stemming both from flexible accumulation and from Toyotist practices that were strongly assimilated by the Brazilian productive sector. Although the Brazilian productive scenario has radically changed, it cannot be said that binomial Taylorism/Fordism has disappeared. On the contrary, whether on the factory floor or in the productive world in a broader sense, a symbiosis seems to be occurring, characterised by a combination of the most intensive elements of Fordism with a deconstructive flexibility rooted in contemporary forms of flexible accumulation and so-called 'lean production'.

A second indication allows us to observe, particularly since the 1990s, a net increase in more deregulated labour relations, distant from labour laws, leading to the creation of a mass of workers who are shifting from the condition of being employed with a work permit to that of being employed without a formal work permit and are thus 'informal' workers in a broad sense.

---

6 Ricardo Antunes, *Riqueza e Miséria do Trabalho no Brasil* (São Paulo: Boitempo, 2006).

By 2010, about 50% of the Brazilian workforce was in this position, deprived of basic employment rights, outside the scope of the social protection system and without a work permit. During the 1980s there were relatively few outsourcing firms and temporary employment agencies in Brazil, but since then that number has increased significantly to meet the huge demand for temporary workers with no employment relationship and formal registration.

It is clear that these changes, linked to the business logic of instrumental rationality, are closely related to the productive restructuring processes of capital, with large companies seeking to increase their competitiveness by further fracturing and fragmenting labour processes (and hence working life) through the flexibilization of labour arrangements, subcontracting and outsourcing.

The increasing extension of such restructuring into services (evidenced by the proliferation of software producers, call centres, telemarketing firms etc.) has brought new groups of workers into this logic of production and value creation, leading to the creation of a new category of workers whom Ursula Huws has called a 'cybertariat',[7] which could also be termed an 'infoproletariat', a new proletariat of the cybernetic age, composed of workers whose labour, involving the use of information and communications technologies, is increasingly virtual, albeit in a profoundly real world.[8]

The stable labour power of the automobile era has shrunk, even while the working-class as a whole has expanded; it has become heterogeneous and complex, which compels us to investigate contemporary forms of labour and value.

3   The New Forms of Labour and Value: Tangibility and Intangibility

With the conversion of living labour into dead labour, from the moment when, through the development of software, the informational machine starts to perform activities that are typical of human intelligence, one can witness what Lojkine suggestively called the 'objectification of brain activity with machinery', the transfer of the intellectual and cognitive knowledge of the working class to computerised machinery.[9] This transfer of intellectual knowledge, which is converted into an informational machine language through computers, emphasises the transformation of living labour into dead labour.

---

7 Ursula Huws, *The Making of a Cybertariat: virtual work in a real world* (New York: Monthly Review Press, 2003).
8 Ricardo Antunes & Ruy Braga (ed.), *Infoproletários: Degradação Real do Trabalho Virtual* (São Paulo: Boitempo, 2009).
9 Jean Lojkine, *A Revolução Informacional* (São Paulo: Editora Cortez, 1995).

This leads to an increasing overlap between tangible and immaterial labour. Alongside the trend for an increasing casualisation of labour already mentioned, there has also been a significant expansion of labour with a greater intellectual dimension, in more highly-computerised industrial activities, in the communications sector and in service employment more generally.

Immaterial labour can thus be said to express the life of the informational sphere of the commodity-form: it is the expression of the informational content of the commodity, thus expressing the mutations of labour within large enterprises and the service sector, where direct manual labour is being replaced by labour endowed with a greater intellectual dimension. With the increasing overlap that exists between them, tangible and immaterial labour are, nevertheless, centrally subordinated to the logic of commodity production and capital. We fully agree here with J. M. Vincent when he says that:

> the form value of labour itself is metamorphosed. It increasingly takes the form value of intellectual-abstract labour. The strength of intellectual labour produced in and out of production is absorbed as a commodity by the capital which is incorporated into it in order to give new qualities to dead labour (...). Tangible production and the production of services increasingly require innovation, thus becoming increasingly subordinated to an increasing production of knowledge to become commodities and capital.[10]

In the era of the 'lean enterprise', the new phase of capital retransfers *savoir faire* to labour, but it does so by increasingly appropriating its intellectual dimension and its cognitive skills, by trying to strongly and intensively involve workers' subjectivity. However, the process is not restricted to this dimension, since part of the intellectual knowledge is transferred to the computerised machines, which become more 'intelligent' by reproducing part of the activities transferred to them through the intellectual knowledge of workers. Since the machine cannot fully eliminate human labour, it requires a greater interaction between the worker's subjectivity and the new intelligent machine.

In this process, interactive involvement further increases the estrangement and alienation of labour, thus expanding modern forms of reification, distancing workers' subjectivity even more from the exercise of what Nicolas Tertulian,

---

10   Jean-Marie Vincent, "Les Automatismes Sociaux et le 'General Intellect'", *Paradigmes du Travail, Futur Antérieur*, no. 16 (1993), 121.

following Lukács, called the exercise of an "authentic and self-determined subjectivity".[11]

So instead of a replacement of labour by science, or even a replacement of production by communication or of production by information, what can be witnessed in the contemporary world is a greater interrelationship, or interpenetration between productive and unproductive activities, between manufacturing and service activities and between manufacturing and design activities, which expand in the context of the productive restructuring of capital. This necessitates the development of an expanded concept for the understanding of labour's way of being in contemporary capitalism, not a denial of labour's continuing relevance.

Theses that argue that the spread of immaterial labour is leading to the end of work, with a consequent imbalance in value, seem misguided.[12] I would argue, on the contrary, that the various forms of immaterial labour express the various forms of living labour that are necessary for the extraction of value in the contemporary world. In the current stage of labour development, in which scientific and job-related experiential knowledge are mixed even more directly than in the past, the creative power of living labour takes both the form (still dominant) of tangible labour and the increasingly important new form of immaterial labour.[13]

Immaterial labour does not become excessive in scale, because, being neither single nor even dominant, immaterial labour is an abstract form of intellectual work, which can be conceived of as a growing number of immaterial 'labour clots' placed in the prevalent logic of tangible accumulation. The measure of value can be given by the average social time of an increasingly complex labour, thus assimilating immaterial workers into the new phase of value production in these new temporal and spatial configurations. The increasing overlap between tangible and immaterial labour should not be seen as dissolving the law of value but rather as creating the preconditions for a new means of analysing value creation in the modern world, in the context of the logic of financialization.

Finally, we must emphasise that if intangibility is a trend, tangibility is still widely prevalent, especially because many of the immaterial activities are condensed and moulded into a set of relationships that end up mostly taking a

---

11   Nicolas Tertulian, "Le Concept d'Aliénation chez Heidegger et Lukács", *Archives de Philosophie: Reserches et Documentation,* no. 56 (1993).
12   André Gorz, *The immaterial* (London: Seagull Books, 2010).
13   Ricardo Antunes, *O Caracol e sua Concha: Ensaios sobre a Nova Morfologia do Trabalho* (São Paulo: Boitempo, 2005).

given tangible form, designed and implemented through a new international division of labour. This is especially visible when capitalism is viewed on a global scale: two thirds of the world's working population can be found in southern countries. China's recent boom (not to mention India's) has been anchored in this enormous labour power surplus – in the incorporation of information technology and the network structure of transnational companies, all articulated with a socio-technical control over workers that has allowed an extreme exploitation of the workforce and, consequently, an immense expansion of value. This process invalidates (both empirically and theoretically) any theory that living labour has become irrelevant in the production of value. These examples also provide evidence of the fragility of arguments that suggest that intangible labour will become predominant and that this will invalidate the law of value.

4 The Design of the New Morphology of Labour

From the intensified labour found in Japan (where young workers migrate in search of work to cities where they sleep in glass capsules, thus becoming truly 'encapsulated' workers) to the contingent labour present in the United States; from the immigrants who migrate to the developed heartlands of the West to the labour underworlds of Asia; from the *maquiladoras* in Mexico to the precarious workforces of Western Europe; from Nike to McDonald's; from General Motors to Ford and Toyota; from global call centres to Walmart workers, whether male or female, a huge variety of forms of living labour may be seen both at the top and the bottom of labour's social structure, all of which participate in one way or another in the total social labour required for the expansion of new forms of value aggregation.

This multifaceted world of work is also characterised both by strong divisions and new transversalities in the workforce, particularly with respect to the dimensions of gender, generation and ethnicity. To give one example, women now form more than 40% of the workforce in Brazil, having been absorbed by capital, mainly in the precarious and unregulated field of part-time labour. This expansion of female labour has a perverse effect in relation to wages and rights, whereby the wage inequality of women contradicts their increased participation in the labour market, because their remuneration rate is much lower than that earned by male labour. There are similar contradictions with respect to labour rights and conditions. The sexual division of labour in contemporary industry typically consigns capital-intensive and design activities to men, with lower-skilled and more labour-intensive tasks being carried out by women, immigrant workers and black people. Women also carry out reproduction work, both paid and unpaid, which is equally essential to capital.[14] Mike Davis reminds us that 'it is not uncommon to find (in Central America) seven- or eight-year-old maids with weekly shifts of ninety working hours and one day off per month'.[15]

With the enormous growth of a new informal proletariat, the industrial and service subproletariat, new jobs are filled by immigrants, such as those known as '*lavoro nero*' in Italy, *Chicanos* in the United States, immigrants from Eastern Europe (Polish, Romanians, Albanians, etc.) in Western Europe, the *Dekasegis* in Japan or the *Bolivianos* in Brazil (who often work 17 hours a day in exchange for food and shelter in the manufacturing companies of São Paulo).

Recent history has given us many reminders of the complex interconnections between labour, unemployment, insecurity and immigration. In the Paris suburbs in late 2005, for instance, this was evident in the upsurge of young people protesting against their status as second-class citizens. In the aftermath of the 2008 crisis (with its epicentres in the USA, Europe and Japan) it was also evident that immigrant workers were among the first to be penalised, both through their direct loss of employment and as a result of a general rise in xenophobia.

In recent decades, there has also been a growth in the inclusion of children in the labour market, particularly in intermediate and subordinate industrialised countries, such as in Asian and Latin American countries, but which also affects several more developed countries. This trend is still very significant in countries like China, India and Brazil. Despite the fact that adults are being laid off and many millions of men and women of working age are experiencing structural unemployment, children are becoming part of the production cycle at a very early age, with their playful bodies precociously transformed into productive capacities for capital. In Brazil the production of sisal, the footwear and clothing industries, the cotton and sugarcane cultures, quarries, coal-pits and brick factories and domestic work provide countless spaces where child labour is exploited by employers. In the textile industry in South Asia, Mike Davis reports, children work in a squatting position for as long as 20 hours a day, and, in the glass industry, work alongside tanks with temperatures close to 1,800 degrees centigrade.[16]

---

14 Anna Pollert, " 'Team work' on the Assembly Line: Contradiction and the Dynamics of Union Resilience", in *The New Workplace and Trade Unionism: Critical Perspectives on Work and Organization*, ed. Peter Ackers, Paul Smith & Chris Smith (London: Routledge, 1996).
15 Mike Davis, *Planet of Slums* (London: Verso, 2017), 188.
16 Ibid., 187.

These examples suggest the complexities of the divisions and transversalities that exist today between stable and precarious workers, between men and women, between the young and the old, between nationals and immigrants, between whites, blacks and indigenous peoples, between the skilled and the unskilled and between the employed and the unemployed. This is the diverse and contradictory reality that makes up the new morphology of labour.

Far from any reduction of the proletariat (as proposed by some univocal theorists) what we are witnessing is the emergence of new and different forms of labour that are spread around the world on a global scale: reconfiguration, and complication of labour and a multiplication of its meanings.

This allows us to conclude by saying that, in an era of labour computerisation and digital accumulation, we are also witnessing an era of labour informalisation, characterised by the expansion of outsourcing, subcontracting, flexibilization, part-time working, teleworking and the growth of a cyberproletariat – a new proletariat working with computers with an experience of work shaped by dematerialisation, insecurity and what, Luciano Vasapollo has called 'atypical work', a 'freeze-dried' workforce that capital is free to draw on and discard at will.[17]

---

17 Vasapollo, *O Trabalho Atípico.*

CHAPTER 7

The Working Class Today

The New Form of Being of the Class-that-lives-from-Labour

Who constitutes the working class today? Does it still maintain its position of centrality in social transformations? These are not simple questions and for decades they have been subject to an avalanche of deconstructions.[1]

The central thesis we seek to develop here is that the centre of social transformation – in the amplified destructive logic of contemporary capitalism – is still mainly rooted in the whole of the working class. From the beginning, we will refute two mistaken theories: that nothing has changed within the workers' universe and, its opposite, that the working class is not capable of radically transforming capitalist society.

It is interesting that, as the number of workers who live by selling their labour power have increased on a global scale, so many authors have waved farewell to the proletariat and have defended the notion of the loss of centrality of the category of labour, or the end of human emancipation through labour.

What I shall demonstrate here is an opposite path. I will attempt a critique of the critique in order to make clear what I have been calling the new morphology of labour and its potentialities.

The definition of the working class today is a central issue. Although it is not identical to the one that existed in the mid-20th century, it is not on the way to extinction nor has ontologically lost its structuring sense in the everyday life of the social being. What then is its current form of being?

We know that both Marx and Engels considered 'working class' and 'proletariat' synonyms. In addition, in the Europe of the mid-19th century, workers that had inspired the reflections of both theorists had acquired bodily expression within the industrial proletariat, which enabled the shared and even undistinguished designation between working class and proletariat.

Our theoretical and political challenge is to understand therefore who is the class-that-lives-from-labour today, and how it is formed.

---

[1] This was first published in *Workers of the World,* vol. 1, no. 2 (2013). Translated by Daila Fanny Eugenio and edited by Murillo van der Laan.

We begin with the idea that it comprises the entire male and female population who live by selling their labour power and who do not possess the means of production, according to the Marxist definition.

Marx designated productive workers as those who formed the core of the working class, especially in the unpublished Chapter 6, *Results of the Direct Production Process*, and in numerous other passages in *Capital*. In these texts the idea of productive labour is elaborated, comprising the productive workers who: produce surplus-value, are paid by money-capital, express a form of collective and social labour, and carry out both material and immaterial labour.[2]

Hence, it becomes clear in our analysis that the working class today does not find itself restricted to direct manual labour, but incorporates the totality of social labour, anyone who sells his or her labour power as a commodity in exchange for a wage.

Therefore, it is still centrally composed of productive workers producing surplus-value who also participate in the process of capital valorisation through the interaction between living and dead labour, between human labour and technological-scientific machinery.

This segment constitutes the central nucleus of the modern proletariat. The products made by Toyota, Nissan, General Motors, IBM, Microsoft, etc. result from the interaction between living and dead labour, making groundless the theses – from Jürgen Habermas[3] to Robert Kurz[4] – that says abstract labour has lost its structuring force in contemporary society.

If abstract labour (the use of physical and intellectual energy to produce commodities, as Marx described in Capital) has lost its structuring force in contemporary society, how are Toyota's cars produced? Who creates Microsoft's software, General Motors' and Nissan's cars, Nike's shoes and McDonalds'

---

2 Karl Marx, "Capital. Volume 1: The Process of Production of Capital", in *Karl Marx & Friedrich Engels, Collected Works, vol. 35* (London: Lawrence & Wishart, 1996); "Chapter Six. Results of the Direct Production Process", *in Karl Marx & Friedrich Engels, Collected Works, vol. 34* (London: Lawrence & Wishart, 1994). See also György Lukács, *Ontologia Dell'Essere Sociale*, I and II (Rome: Riuniti, 1976, 1981) and Ernest Mandel, "Marx, La Crise Actuelle et L'Avenir du Travail Humain", *Quatrième Internationale*, no. 2 (1986), 9–29.

3 Jürgen Habermas, "Technology and Science as 'Ideology' ", in *Toward a Rational Society: Student Protest, Science, and Politics* (Boston: Beacon Press, 1989); "The New Obscurity", in *The New Conservatism: Cultural Criticism and the Historians' Debate* (Cambridge: Polity Press, 1989); *The Theory of Communicative Action vol. 1: Reason and the Rationalization of Society* (London: Polity Press, 1991); *The Theory of Communicative Action vol. 2: The Critique of Functionalist Reason* (London: Polity Press, 1992).

4 Robert Kurz, *Der Kollaps der Modernisierung: vom Zusammenbruch des Kasernen Sozialismus zur Krise der Weltokonomie* (Frankfurt am Main: Vito von Eichborn GmbH & Co. Verlag, 1991); *Os Últimos Combates* (Rio de Janeiro: Vozes, 1997).

hamburgers? – to mention just a few examples from prominent transnational corporations.

We advance here to a second important element: the working class also includes unproductive workers, again in Marx's understanding of the term; that is, those whose forms of labour are used as services, both for public use, such as traditional public services, and for capital's use. Unproductive labour is labour that does not constitute itself as a living element in the process of capital valorisation and the creation of surplus value. This is why Marx differentiates it from productive labour, which participates directly in the process of creating surplus value.

As the real differences are blurred – it is enough to recall that in the sphere of production today the same work can include productive and unproductive tasks, carried out by the same worker – the amplified working class includes, therefore, the broad array of unproductive wage-earners, anti-value producers within the capitalist labour process, who experience, however, situations clearly similar to those experienced by productive workers. As the real differences are blurred – it is enough to recall that in the sphere of production today the same work can include productive and unproductive tasks, carried out by the same worker – the amplified working class includes, therefore, the broad array of unproductive wage-earners, anti-value producers within the capitalist labour process, who experience, however, situations clearly similar to those experienced by productive workers. They belong to what Marx called the "overhead costs of production" that are, however, completely vital to the survival of capitalism and its social metabolism.

Given that all productive labour is waged ('exceptions' aside, such as the resurgence of slave labour) but not all wage labour is productive, a contemporary understanding of the working class must include all wage-earners.

Therefore, the working class today is broader, more heterogeneous, more complex and more fragmented than the industrial proletariat of the nineteenth and early twentieth centuries.

An important question to our debate remains: does the modern proletariat that executes productive activities (whether predominantly material or immaterial activities; made manually or using the information technology of the most advanced modern factories, which demands activities considered more 'intellectualized') still have a central role in anti-capitalist struggles, precisely because it creates exchange values and surplus value? Or conversely, does the amplified modern proletariat or the class-that-lives-from-labour not have any necessary core – considering its heterogeneity and participation/production/amplification of value, as well as its concrete ideological-political reality?

Reformulating: in the conflicts led by workers all around the world, is it possible to detect a greater role and potential amongst the more skilled strata of the working class, in those living under 'more stable' conditions and who therefore participate to a greater extent in the process of value-creation? Or conversely, are the more fertile poles of action found precisely amongst the most marginalized, sub-proletarianised strata?

We know that the more skilled, more intellectualized segments which advanced along with technological-informational-digital development, given their central role in the creation of exchange-values, could be endowed, at least objectively, with greater potential for rebellion.

On the other hand, and paradoxically, these more skilled segments are experiencing a systematic process of manipulation and 'involvement' (which are actually contemporary forms of fetishism and estrangement) within the workplace. In contrast, the broad array of precarious, part-time, temporary, etc., workers – the so-called modern subproletariat, – along with the huge contingent of the unemployed, due to their greater distance from the process of value-creation, would have, at a material level, a less important role in anti-capitalist struggles. Yet the condition of dispossession leads them to daily confrontations with the destructive order, since they have nothing else to lose in capital's universe of (un)sociability. Their subjectivity could be, therefore, more prone to lead to rebellion.

It is always worth remembering that the working class is a condition of particularity, a form of being, carrying clear, intrinsic and non-eliminable relational elements of objectivity and subjectivity.

The working class for Marx is ontologically decisive due to its fundamental role in the process of value creation and class struggle. It is in the very materiality of the system and in the workers' subjective potential that its role becomes central. The working class will only lose this potentiality if and when abstract labour no longer plays a central role in the reproduction of capital.

In a broader sense, the working class thus includes all those selling their labour power in exchange for a wage, such as the rural proletariat that sells its labour power to capital, for example – the so-called bóias-frias of Brazil's ethanol and agro-industrial regions. Moreover, we may include the growing part-time industrial and service-sector proletariat, characterized by temporary contracts and precarious working conditions. The working class also embraces – in a decisive manner today – unemployed workers.

The issue of immigration is perhaps one of the most emblematic features of capitalism. Given the sharp rise of the new informal proletariat and of the manufacturing and service-sector subproletariat, new jobs are performed by immigrant labour, such as the Gastarbeiters in Germany, the lavoratori in nero in

Italy, the chicanos in the United States, Eastern European immigrants (Polish, Hungarian, Romanian, Albanian workers) in West Europe, the Dekasegis of Japan, the Bolivians/Latin-Americans and Africans in Brazil, Argentina, etc.

Our concept of the working class excludes managers of capital, who constitute a portion of the dominant class due to the important role they play in the control, hierarchy, command and management of capital and in its processes of valorisation; small-business owners; urban and rural propertied bourgeoisie that hold – even if on a small scale – the means of production. Also excluded are those who live by means of speculation and interest.

Therefore, a broader understanding of the working class today entails a comprehension of this heterogeneous, amplified, complex and fragmented set of social beings that live from the sale of their labour power, wage earners deprived of the means of production.

Under Taylorism/Fordism during the 20th century, workers were not homogeneous: there had always been male workers, female workers, young workers, skilled and unskilled workers, native and immigrant workers, etc., i.e. multiple variations within the working class. Clearly at that time there was also outsourcing (in general, such as in catering, cleaning and public transport). But in the last decades we have witnessed a huge intensification of this process that has qualitatively affected the structure of the working class, increasing and intensifying the already existing divergences.

Unlike Taylorism/Fordism (which, it is important to remember, still exists in many parts of the world, albeit in a hybrid or mixed form), under Toyotism or flexible accumulation processes, workers are internalized and encouraged to become their own despots, as shown in Part 1. They are oriented by notions of self-incrimination and self-punishment if their production does not reach the well-known 'targets'. They work in teams or production-cells, and if one of them does not turn up to work, he/she is supposed to justify himself/herself to members of the team. This is how things work, for instance, in the ideal of Toyotism. Resistance, rebellion and denial are completely opposed by managers, regarded as acts against the 'good performance of the company'.

If within the Taylorist/Fordist system, scientific management plan and the manual labourer executes, under Toyotism and flexible lean-production forms, intellectual knowledge is allowed to blossom and worker subjectivity is appropriated by capital.

This expansive and complex process within the sectors at the cutting edge of the production process (which by no means can be generalized nowadays), results in more intelligent machines, which in turn have to be operated by 'skilled' workers, more capable of operating computerised machines. Throughout this process, new smarter machines perform activities, which were previously done solely by humans, creating an interactive process between distinctive living labour and computerised dead labour.

This prompted Habermas to say misleadingly that science has become the leading productive force, making the labour theory of value superfluous. On the contrary, I believe in a new interaction between living and dead labour; there is a process of the technologization of science (in the concept of Mészáros[5]) which, however, cannot eliminate living labour in the process of value creation. Indeed, there is considerable evidence that, parallel to the rise of new forms of labour, there are new modalities in which the law of value operates.

In fact, we are witnessing the growth and expansion of forms of the creation of surplus value, resulting from the articulation of highly advanced machinery (exemplified by communication and information technologies invading the commodity sphere), with capital demanding a more 'skilled' and 'competent' workforce.

Given the new morphology of labour and its huge range of invisible workers, value-creating mechanisms have been potentialized, although under a non-value appearance, using new and old mechanisms of the intensification of work (if not through the very self-exploration of labour).

Our hypothesis thus goes in the opposite direction of those who claim that the labour theory of value is no longer valid (as do Habermas, Kurz and Gorz[6]): it states that labour invisibility is an apparent expression that conceals the real creation of surplus value within almost all spheres of the world of work where exploitation takes place. Therefore, contrary to the elaborations that deconstruct the labour theory of value, there has been an important expansion and reinforcement of surplus value creation in contemporary capitalism.

Otherwise, why would there currently be a 17-hour shift in the clothing industry of São Paulo, Brazil, performed by Bolivian or Peruvian (or other Latin-American) immigrant workers, usually informally hired and controlled by Korean or Chinese employers? Or African workers packing textile and clothing products in Bom Retiro and Brás neighbourhoods in São Paulo? Those products are sold in the African market, created by an arduous and mainly manual labour, as documented by the workers themselves. Here, examples from the agribusiness sector abound. The average amount of sugarcane cut in the state of São Paulo by one worker is ten tons per day, whereas the average amount in the Northeastern region of Brazil can reach 18 tons per day.

---

5   István Mészáros, *The Power of Ideology* (London: Harvester Wheatsheaf, 1989); *Beyond Capital: Towards a Theory of Transition* (London: Merlin Press, 1995).
6   Habermas, "Technology and Science as 'Ideology' "; Kurz, *Der Kollaps der Modernisierung*; André Gorz, *The immaterial* (London: Seagull Books, 2010).

In Japan, for instance, young workers migrating to the big cities looking for jobs spend the night in glass capsules; as a result, I have called them 'encapsulated' workers. Furthermore, there are the cyber-refugees, young workers in Tokyo who do not have money to rent rooms; they use cybercafés to rest and look for work. The cybercafés on the outskirts of Tokyo have special prices for workers willing to spend the night searching for contingent jobs on the Internet.

Once the informalization of labour, in its polymorphic design, becomes more permanent and structural, it seems to increasingly assume the distinctive mark of capital accumulation in contemporary society.

There is a new working-class contingent booming: information and communication technology workers, encompassing software producers to call centre and telemarketing staff. These workers are part of the new morphology of labour, and have been designated 'cybertariat' (Huws[7]) or 'infoproletariat' (Antunes and Braga[8]).

As we know, the global privatization of telecommunications and the search for more profitability in these companies have unleashed the increasing practice of outsourcing, resulting in multiple new ways of making time and movement in labour processes more precarious and intense.

It is worth remembering that labour within the information and communication technology sectors is contradictorily structured; it aligns 21st century technologies to 20th century working conditions. Similarly, it combines strategies of intense emulation and involvement, as in the Toyotised flexible system, with Taylorist/Fordist management techniques.

Therefore, contrary to the analysis of critics of labour and the law of value as the bases of the capitalist society, it is possible to say that new modalities of labour, including immaterial labour, have arisen as expressions of the living labour that participate in value accumulation. Once science and labour are directly blended in the sphere of production, the creative power of labour can assume both the dominant form of material labour or the tendential modality of immaterial labour, since the very creation of advanced digital-computerised machinery results from the active interaction between the intellectual knowledge of labour and computerised machines. In this process, some of the predicates of the intellectual knowledge of labour are transferred

---

[7] Ursula Huws, *The Making of a Cybertariat: virtual work in a real world* (New York: Monthly Review Press, 2003).
[8] Ricardo Antunes & Ruy Braga, ed., *Infoproletários: Degradação Real do Trabalho Virtual* (São Paulo: Boitempo, 2009). See also Luciano Vasapollo, *O Trabalho Atípico e a Precariedade* (São Paulo: Expressão Popular, 2005).

to the new computerised machines and thus, subjective activities are objectified (Lojkine[9]) or become "organs of the human brain, created by the human hand", as Marx characterised in the Grundrisse,[10] providing new dimensions and aspects to the labour theory of value. When the cognitive dimension of labour is aroused by production, it becomes a constitutive part of the globally existent complex, combining with social labour.

Thus, in our analysis, when the immaterial form of labour and production occurs, it does not lead to the extinction of the law of value, but adds living labour clots within the logic of capital accumulation, in its materiality, inserting them into the average social time of an increasingly complex labour process. Contrary to the breakdown of the law of value, it is therefore mandatory to unveil the new value creating mechanisms, pertaining to the informational sphere of the commodity-form.[11] It is worth remembering Toyota's Takaoka plant, where the following slogan is found outside its premises: "Yoi kangae, yoi shina" (Good thoughts equal good products).[12] In addition, the boom of China and India during the last decades, based on the enormous extra labour power and the incorporation of information technologies, seems to invalidate the thesis of the loss of relevance of living labour in the sphere of value creation. It increases the fragility of arguments that say immateriality demonstrates the inadequacy of the law of value.

Finally, the design of the new morphology of labour configures itself in a more complex way within the real world. Globally speaking, at the top of the social pyramid we find highly skilled jobs in the digital computerised sphere, at the bottom, the structural expansion of precarious conditions and unemployment. In the middle, the hybrid form, the skilled labour that can potentially disappear or erode and thus become precarious and/or unemployed, due to (temporal and spatial) changes in the production. All these social segments are ruled by the growing informality of forms of being.

Thus, besides current diversities and transversalities related to the stable and precarious, male and female, young and old, white, black and indigenous, skilled and unskilled, employed and unemployed workers – and so many other

---

9   Jean Lojkine, *A Revolução Informacional* (São Paulo: Editora Cortez, 1995).
10 Karl Marx, "Outlines of the Critique of Political Economy" in *Karl Marx & Friedrich Engels, Collected Works, vol. 29* (London: Lawrence & Wishart, 1987), 92.
11 André Tosel, "Centralité et Non-Centralité du Travail ou La Passion des Hommes Superflus", in *La Crise du Travail. Actuel Marx Confrontation*, ed. Jacques Bidet & Jacques Texier (Paris: Presses Universitaries de France, 1995); Jean-Marie Vincent, "Les Automatismes Sociaux et le 'General Intellect' ", *Paradigmes du Travail, Futur Antérieur*, no. 16 (1993).
12 *Business Week*, 18 November, 2003.

examples that constitute the new morphology of labour – immigrant workers best illustrate this global trend of a precarious labour structure.

It is worth adding a brief note for its symbolic meaning: in Portugal there is a precarious workers' movement called 'Precári@s Inflexíveis' [Inflexible Precarious Workers]. In their Manifesto, this association states:

> We are precarious in work and in life. We work without contract or on short-term contracts. [We have] temporary, uncertain jobs, without guarantees. We are call centre workers, interns, unemployed people, independent workers, immigrant workers, casual workers, student-workers [...] We are not represented in statistics [...] We live off filler jobs. We can hardly provide a home. We can't take leave; we can't have children or become sick. Not to mention the right to strike. 'Flexicurity'? The 'flexi' is for us, while the 'security' is for our bosses. This 'modernization' is tricky and it has been planned and implemented by businessmen and Government, hand in hand. We are in the shadows but we are not silent. We won't stop fighting for fundamental rights alongside the workers in Portugal or abroad. This struggle is not about trade-union or government statistics [...] We don't fit in those figures. We won't let our conditions be forgotten. And using the same force with which we are attacked by our bosses, we will respond and reinvent our struggle. In the end, there are many more of us than of them. Yes, we are precarious, but we are inflexible.[13]

This is therefore the new morphology of labour today. To comprehend its form of being, its attitudes, rebellions and resistances is a path for a better perception of the current multiple and polysemous anti-capitalist struggle.

13 "Manifesto Precário", Precári@s Inflexíveis, Accessed 10 October 2020, http://www.precarios.net/manifesto-precario/.

CHAPTER 8

The Crisis Seen Globally

Robert Kurz and the Collapse of Modernization

Unfortunately, on July 18th, 2012, the German critic Robert Kurz unexpectedly passed away, after a surgery recently carried out.[1] Despite being largely unknown in many parts of the European continent, Robert Kurz was responsible for one of the most creative and radical critiques of capitalism and its 'commodity-producing system', to mention one of his key-concepts. Founder of the journals *Krisis* and *Exit!*, highly influenced by Marx's critique of political economy and the theory of commodity fetishism, Kurz wrote extensively. His book *Der Kollaps der Modernisierung: vom Zusammenbruch des Kasernen Sozialismus zur Krise der Weltokonomie* (*The Collapse of Modernization: From the Fall of Barracks Socialism to World Economic Crisis*) is perhaps the most emblematic and well known of his large body of work.[2]

The critical note that follows has a dual purpose: to present a review of his book mentioned above and at the same time to remember and pay a modest tribute to one of the most important contemporary critics of capital.

1   An Explosive Book

We are before a book with a very strong impact. At first, it seems difficult to review it because, on one hand, it is highly convincing. However, on the other hand, it is also problematic, sometimes even insufficient. Its first dimension, highly positive, is stronger than its second. It is a privileged book, a rare event in an age of almost absolute conformism and resignation, of enchantment with the values of capital and the market. In other words, it is an age of the cult of indetermination, of estrangement, of fetishization, of the end of history and many other manifestations of dominant irrationality.

---

1 This was translated by Josué Pereira da Silva and edited by Murillo van der Laan.
2 This book, written originally in German by Robert Kurz, was published as *Der Kollaps der Modernisierung: vom Zusammenbruch des Kasernensozialismus zur Krise der Weltokonomie* (Frankfurt am Mein: Vito von Eichborn GmbH & Co. Verlag KG, 1991) and in Brazil as *O Colapso da Modernização: Da Derrocada do Socialismo de Caserna à Crise da Economia Mundial* (São Paulo: Paz e Terra, 1992). The references here are from the Brazilian edition.

The book defends its central thesis with vigour and force: the fall of Eastern Europe and of the so-called socialist countries was not an expression of the victory of capitalism and of the West, but a manifestation of a particular crisis which now fulminates the heart of the world commodity-producing system. It was, then, a moment of the global crisis of capital, which had begun in the Third World, affected the European countries in a demolishing manner, and now deeply penetrates the centre of the commodity mode of production and of the society of abstract labour.

In Kurz's own words:

> the 'planned market' of the East [...] did not eliminate the categories of the market. Consequently, all the fundamental categories of capitalism appeared in actually existing socialism: wage, price and profit (the enterprises' earnings). Moreover, the basic principle of abstract labour was not only adopted but also carried out to its extreme.[3]

The countries of the East were part "of the proper commodity-producing system", being just a variation of the latter and never something effectively new and socialist. The ones who take the statism of the East as a starting point to differentiate it from capitalism forget the fact that, in various moments of its constitution and consolidation, the capitalist social formation requested the protection of the state.

Thus, Mercantilism, the Age of Bismarck and Keynesian interventionism are all examples, according to Kurz, of this recurrence to the state. Suggestive and highly provocative in his theoretical indications and conclusions, though also enormously a-historical, Kurz tries to show how the "statism of the actually existing socialism" has, in fact, many similarities with the rational bourgeois state of Fichte as well as with Mercantilism. For him, institutions such as planned market, right to work and state monopoly of international trade, all present in actually existing socialism,

> were pre-formulated by capitalism itself and by its progressive ideologists at the threshold of industrialization. Thus, they are in their essence not strange to capital or to the commodity-producing system; they are rather structural characteristics of the historical formation of the latter.[4]

---

3 Kurz, *O Colapso da Modernização*, 29.
4 Ibid., 42.

The cult of abstract labour, taken to its limit in the East, shows how the Marxian critique of fetishism was completely out of consideration, "eliminated and pushed to a purely theoretical and historical dimension, discredited as obscure, or degraded as a purely subjective mental phenomenon".[5]

Without internally breaking with the logic of the commodity-producing system, the

> crisis of the work-based society of the actually existing socialism marks the imminent crisis of the modern society of work in general. This was so precisely because the mechanisms of competition triumphed and, in fact, undermined and debilitated the foundations of the commodity-producing system. It is part of the logic of this system the fact that its weakest components, in terms of productivity and interlacement, are the first to fall into the abyss of the collapsing system [...].[6]

We can see that the author conceives the crisis of modernity in its global dimension. Without the principle of competition, absolutely unproductive and obsolete in its technological development, the East simultaneously saw the germination of a society of scarcity and waste. When the West experienced a significant technological boom through microelectronics during the 1970s and 1980s, the competition and the logic of the world commodity-producing system ended up contributing to the complete collapse of the "actually existing socialism", which "had to fail in its own internal rationality, in the commodity-form carried out to an extreme absurdity and in the untenable relationship with the external world [...]".[7]

Thus, the post-1989 transition, experienced by the USSR and the East, is not to be compared with the advanced West, but with the closer reality of the Third World. The latter, on the other extreme of the global crisis of the commodity-producing system, already constitutes what the author calls "post-catastrophic societies":

> [...] the Third World either has already failed in its modernization attempt (...) or, at best, found a precarious status, in the role of ascending countries, which remains exposed to the Damocles' sword of the world market and, even so, without the possibility of internal development for the whole society.[8]

---

5   Ibid., 48.
6   Ibid., 90.
7   Ibid., 152.
8   Ibid., 176.

The few exceptions of 'export-oriented industrialization', exemplified by Asian countries like South Korea, Hong Kong, Taiwan and Singapore, remain in a "precarious dependence on the Western countries" and have not experienced, until now, the development of an internal market capable of providing a solid basis for these industrializing projects. Moreover, these are in their majority small and insular countries, whose industrializing projects can hardly be feasible in continental countries:

> the insular industrial structure which is capable of competing in the world market is unilaterally oriented to export, and the internal market cannot be sufficiently developed because the apparently successful experience of industrialization directed to export cannot generate the sufficient volume of internal acquisitive capacity, due to its high intensity of capital. The decisive factor in this process is not low wages, but rather the inability of these highly automatized productions to absorb a sufficient mass of the labour force.[9]

For the Third World, Kurz can visualize only social rebellions, movements inspired by fundamentalism, always subjected to the intervention of an "international police power" supported by the United Nations. Losing their role of furnishers of abundant and underpaid labour force to productive capital and being out of the technological competition at the centre of the system, these countries are clear expressions of the other extreme of the collapse.

Kurz's conclusion is sharp:

> the logic of the crisis is running from the periphery to the centre. After the collapses of the Third World in the 1980s and of the actually existing socialism in the beginning of the 1990s, it is now the time of the West.[10]

The same unequal logic which regulated the relations between the central countries and the Third World also penetrates the Western logic.

> what marks the next phase is that whole regions are 'running out', they are perishing as industrial regions because they were defeated in the competition of the world markets and are no longer able to raise monetary capital to continue in the productivity race.[11]

---

9   Ibid., 176.
10   Ibid., 206.
11   Ibid., 211.

Here Kurz is referring to the core countries of the system: the USA and England "are dissipating their own resources of monetary capital in a consumption that is unproductive on the level of world powers", consumption that could no longer be put into practice.[12] For Japan and Germany, the 'winners', there is no possibility of escaping the driving force of this destructive logic: "For many years and in unimaginable dimensions", they have been financing

> their success in exporting to world markets, lending to the OECD economies – which have in fact been defeated in the competition – the resources necessary to continue 'flooding' them with imported commodities. That is the only reason why the economies within the OECD that lost have not yet taken the course of the post-catastrophic societies of the South and of the East, at the price of accumulating an enormous amount of unsolvable debt.[13]

The author's conclusion is clear: we are entering an era of darkness, of unforeseeable consequences. And

> since this crisis precisely consists of the tendential elimination of productive labour (…), no longer can it be criticized or even superseded from the ontological point of view of 'work', of the 'working class ', or of the 'struggle of the working classes'.[14]

Marxism (together with the labour movement) is itself an "integral part of the bourgeois world of the modern commodity, being also, for that reason, affected by the crisis".[15] Despite his enormous recovery of Marxian formulations, at this point Kurz's only (and strong) criticism of Marx appears:

> no doubt, a dilemma, up to now unresolved, arises at the centre of Marx's theory. The affirmation of the labour movement (…) is in fact irreconcilable with its own critique of political economy, which precisely unmasks the working class understood not as an ontological category, but rather as a social category constituted, by its turn, by capital.[16]

---

12   Ibid.
13   Ibid., 213.
14   Ibid., 227.
15   Ibid.
16   Ibid., 71.

The labour movement, according to Kurz, has conducted the *capitalist* emancipation of workers, but it is not the subject capable of advancing social emancipation. With another provocative and audacious thesis, he completed his essay arguing that

> the supposedly unsuccessful Communism, which is mistaken by the collapsing societies of the recuperative modernization, is neither a utopia nor a distant goal, never to be arrived at, far beyond reality; it is, on the contrary, a phenomenon already present, in fact, the closest we find, even in its wrong and negative form, within the capitalist involucres of the world commodity-producing system, i.e., in the form of a communism of things, as the global interlacing of the content of human reproduction.[17]

Given the impossibility and inexistence of a collective subject capable of overcoming the crisis, within the universe of the world of work, Kurz delineates his proposition: it becomes necessary to search for "a sensitive reason, which is exactly the opposite of the Reason of the Enlightenment, which is abstract, bourgeois and linked to the commodity form".[18] This radical criticism "would have to completely emancipate itself from its former obsolete ideas"; however, the "left, in all its colours, appears completely incapable of giving a response to the crisis".[19]

2 And Its Main Gaps

As we tried to show in these pages through an immanent analysis, Kurz's essay is polemical and problematic. It is a text where priority is given to the ontology, where the apprehension of the logic of the object – the contemporary crisis of the commodity-producing system, of capitalism – is followed in its essential and totalizing nexus. In sum, we can say that his formulations are essentially correct in regard to the diagnosis of the crisis of capital of our days, but they fail in prefiguring and proposing a way to go beyond capital. Maybe this is too much to demand nowadays. After all, it is no doubt an unusual and strong claim to visualize the defeat of capitalism from the analysis of the collapse of Eastern Europe. Moreover, it is rather uncommon to demonstrate this by means of a vigorous and suggestive recovery of the Marxian critique of political economy.

---

[17] Ibid., 228.
[18] Ibid., 232.
[19] Ibid., 226–227.

It is also a strong quality of this instigating book, the fact that it allows us to reflect and rethink, from the left, on many 'unquestionable' points. However, I would like to conclude this review by pointing out some of the problems that arose from its reading.

First critique: in his ontological recuperation of the object, Kurz suppressed the dimension of subjectivity, which is decisive in Marx. The beings and characters of capital and labour are epiphenomena of a logic given by a strong objectivism. At this point, as the provocative tone of the text suggests, it seems to us that Kurz's materialism is closer to Feuerbach than to Marx. It is worth to remember here the first thesis on Feuerbach:

> the chief defect of all previous materialisms (that of Feuerbach included) is that things [Gegenstand], reality, sensuousness are conceived only in the form of the object, or of contemplation, but not as sensuous human activity, practice, not subjectively. [20]

The lacuna Kurz attributes to Marx is in fact his own; his understanding of fetishism as something almost integral and irremovable prevents the active existence and the effective resistance of the subjects. Here Kurz pays an unnecessary price to the critics of the labouring society, to whom he approximates and from whom he differs as well.

Close to Habermas (and indirectly to Gorz and Offe), Kurz places himself into the universe of the critiques of the centrality of work in the contemporary world. With the substantial difference that, for him, the issue is to eliminate the centrality of abstract labour, as it was the case also for Marx since the time he had prepared the Manuscripts of 1844. For Marx, however, it is indispensable to recover the concrete dimension of labour as a vital activity, as the source which creates socially necessary use values, or to remember the old Lukács, as *proto-form of human activity*.

Kurz is not sufficiently clear in this regard (which is a lacuna), but he suggests a relevant path in the following paragraph:

> the society of work as an ontological concept would be a tautology since, in all of history up to now, the social life, in all its modified form could only be a life which included work. Only the naive ideas of the paradise and the tales of wonderland could fantasize a society without work.[21]

---

20   Karl Marx, "Theses on Feuerbach", in *Karl Marx & Friedrich Engels, Collected Works, vol. 5* (London: Lawrence & Wishart, 1976), 3.
21   Kurz, *O Colapso da Modernização*, 26.

Despite this reference, Kurz seems still partially tributary to the defenders of the crisis of labouring society. Putting it clearly: one thing is the exhaustion of the abstract labour society, another, very different, is the critique that refuses a societal project which conceives work as the creator of use values, in its concrete dimension, as de-fetishized vital activity, as the starting point (not the arriving point) to human omnilaterality.

Kurz concentrates all of his analysis on the prevalence of the destructive and generalized production of commodities and, consequently, on the Marxian labour theory of value; once we reaffirm the actuality of this thesis (which is another enormous quality of the book), it seems difficult to deny the objective existence of the contradiction within the process of valorisation of capital. Thus, the objective struggle between the totality of social labour and the totality of capital does not contradict the Marxian critique of political economy; on the contrary, it is absolutely essential to it. They are not "two completely differing historical logics", as Kurz assumes, but rather intrinsic moments of the same logic, of the class which creates values and, precisely for that reason, has the possibility to rebel and oppose capital.

If the labour theory of value is valid, class struggle becomes its inevitable consequence. Moreover, this was one of the central ontological acquisitions of Marx who, in the *Introduction* to the *Critique of Hegel's Philosophy of Right* (1844), preliminarily conceived the proletariat as the "class with radical chains" and later as the one that sells the "commodity labour power which creates values" and, for this reason, experiences the real possibility of the contradiction facing capital. This essential point brings the discussion to the universe of the subjective limitations of the world of labour, a thematic field refused by Kurz, as we have seen.

His criticism that, in this century, the labour movement has increasingly been linked to the struggle within the universe of the commodities society is to a certain extent true, mainly if we consider the enormous limitations of the so-called traditional left. Nevertheless, this is not enough to enable Kurz to rule out the total absence of subjects. For Marx it was always clear that "the proletariat [...] is compelled as proletariat to abolish itself", if the goal is actually to supersede the society of capital (Marx, *The Holy Family*). Thus, and if we want to dwell on the essence of the discussion Kurz raises, the class-that-lives-from-labour is not objectively unable to supersede capitalism (as Kurz holds), though it can only do that if its self-consciousness incorporates, as a decisive moment, its self-abolition as a class – the moment of the species-being for-itself. It is, we have to admit, a monumental task, which, we think, only a radical, critical and renewed social left, with a clear Marxian inspiration and forged within the world of work, is able to achieve. Both the traditional left (of the Stalinist era) and the Social Democratic left are incapable of carrying out this task.

Second Critique: if the continuity between the East and the West is true in the sense that both are placed in the universe of the commodity-producing system, this does not allow a complete identification between what has occurred in the post-capitalist countries and in the capitalist ones. Kurz speaks of 'socialism of barracks', 'actually existing socialism', 'pre-bourgeois transitory regime', late Mercantilism, among other denominations. Considerable conceptual imprecision shows up here. We don't believe that the Russian Revolution was bourgeois in its origins, as Kurz argues, but that it saw its own developmental process bending, little by little, in an increasing manner, to the logic of world capital. Kurz contributes a lot to reaffirm and demonstrate this latter thesis.

Third Critique: Kurz has a good amount of reason in linking the Marxism of the 20th century to the tragedy of Eastern Europe. However, he exaggerates, and on several points, he is wrong. Observe the two following examples in this regard: to say that "Trotsky could, in the first place, become another Stalin"[22] is only acceptable when the empire of objectivity is so oversized that it suppresses all of the subjective dimension. Here again Kurz is closer to Feuerbach than to Marx. The same is true when he says that nothing is to be saved of Western Marxism, "if we abstract some isolated initiatives, which are unclear and without further result." This ended up being the reason for the "absence of a critique of fetishism".[23]

From the 'reification' present in *History and Class Consciousness* to the vigorous theory of estrangement found in the *Ontology of Social Being*, this was Lukács' enormous undertaking, which certainly was not "unclear and without further result." The same could be said of Gramsci, who reinvigorated contemporary Marxism, because he understood the subjective dimension, the political mediation, the emancipating dimension of culture, etc., not as epiphenomena reducible to a strong objectivism. In this point Kurz is too arrogant. To undertake a critique of the political, understanding it as mediation, as Marx does, is not to disregard it, as Kurz does, or to treat it as a mere epiphenomenon.

Fourth Critique: Kurz redraws the collapse of the money-commodity producing society. He does not see an emancipating exit carried out by the force of labour. He does not consider the hypothesis of a conservative (re)action of the bourgeois forces seeking to minimize the crisis, in so doing prolonging the

---

22   Ibid., 50.
23   Ibid., 49.

sociability governed by capital. We believe, on the contrary, that both alternatives are present: the reaction of capital, trying to soften the age of darkness, preventing that the brave world of money collapse.

Expanded structural unemployment, just to cite an example, becomes a problem for the subjects of capital when it causes an accentuated depression in the consumption market to the point of endangering the realization of capital's valorisation process.

The other alternative is labour's praxis. Under the ruin of the disastrous experience of the East, labour can, perhaps for the first time in this century, look at the West and the world, and see itself being undermined by capital's destructive logic. Then, it can dare in a critical, renewed and radical manner, to go beyond capital, dispensing "all the rules of the so-called world civilization", since

> these democratic rules of the bourgeois and enlightened reason are abstract and insensitive in their essence, their true foundation being the self-movement of money, which is abstract and deprived of meaning [...].[24]

Last point: it is a shame that Robert Kurz, a very interesting author responsible for one of the most damning critiques of capitalism and its destructive effects, was incapable of understanding the new configurations of class struggle, which are not the 'last battles', but the new forms of confrontation between labour as a whole and total social capital, between the working class, in its various cleavages, and the personifications of capital. Although his critique of European trade unionism is largely vivid and true – "trade union protest [...] does not seriously imagine [...] even the outline of an alternative system [...]" – Kurz has, on the other hand, great difficulty grasping class-movements that transcend the sphere of traditional trade unionism. He sees them as the expression of the "old class-struggle" that has been overcome, which "can only be the immanent formal movement of the capital relation, but not the movement that can overcome the capitalist relation". And in doing so, he is imprisoned in the denunciation of the contemporary destructive chaos, devoid of subjects.

Kurz's book *The Collapse of Modernization* is an inspiring effort and a lively reflection. Nonconformist and anticapitalistic as it is, in certain ways it sometimes goes beyond and contradicts some of its own formulations. It constitutes

---

24 Ibid., 199.

an expressive analysis and a response to our current situation, coming from a subjectivity that was not subordinated to the values of capital and to the estrangements often cultivated today. Written as a sharp essay against the logic and the contemporary mechanisms of capital's sociability, this book succeeds in being of great impact.

CHAPTER 9

The International Working Class in 1864 and Today

1   Introduction[1]

The *International Workingmen's Association* (IWA) was born in London on September 28, 1864. Its founders, together with Marx, were a distinguished group of communist, socialist and anarchist intellectuals and activists, who dedicated to the project an important part of their lives.

The history of the IWA, which lasted only until 1876, was short but seminal. During the era of formation of the world market, it was necessary to bring together the various working-class organizations from different parts of the world, so that they could share their experiences of struggle and weave ties of solidarity. As capital acquired global contours, so also should the working-class movement. The working class would need to become organically international, capable of exerting power at an international level while at the same time respecting the distinctive features of each of its national components. This was the *leitmotif* underlying the IWA.

Already in its inaugural manifesto, the First International noted the increasing impoverishment of the working-class:

> It is a great fact that the misery of the working masses has not diminished from 1848 to 1864, and yet this period is unrivalled for the development of its industry and the growth of its commerce.[2]

Given this hard reality, the nascent international movement recognized the urgent necessity of developing a political economy of labour in opposition to the political economy of capital. As stated by Marx in the inaugural manifesto:

> [...] to bear fruit, the means of labour need not be monopolized as a means of dominion over, and of extortion against, the labouring man himself;
> [...] like slave labour, like serf labour, hired labour is but a transitory and

---

[1] This was first published in *Socialism and Democracy,* vol. 28, no. 2 (2014). Translated by Daila Fanny Eugenio and Victor Wallis.

[2] Karl Marx, "Inaugural Address of the International Working Men's Association, The First International", in *Karl Marx & Friedrich Engels, Collected Works*, vol. 20 (London: Lawrence & Wishart, 1976), 5.

inferior form, destined to disappear before associated labour plying its toil with a willing hand, a ready mind, and a joyous heart.[3]

The First International thus pronounced in its Statutes the essential principle, "the emancipation of the working-classes must be conquered by the working-classes themselves". Further,

> the economical emancipation of the working-classes is therefore the great end to which every political movement ought to be subordinate. [...] All societies and individuals adhering to it will acknowledge truth, justice, and morality as the basis of their conduct toward each other and toward all men, without regard to colour, creed, or nationality.[4]

The General Council of the IWA would act as an international organ linking "the different co-operating associations, so that the working men in one country be consistently informed of the movements of their class in every other country." And, "when immediate practical steps should be needed, as, for instance, in case of international quarrels, the action of the associated societies [would] be simultaneous and uniform". Nonetheless, "While united in a perpetual bond of fraternal co-operation, the working men's societies joining the International Association, will preserve their existent organizations intact".[5]

If these were the goals of the IWA 150 years ago, what does it mean to think of an international organization of the working class today? Would its most general principles become dated? Or would they, on the contrary, become even more relevant? If today's working-class needs an international organization, how can we imagine what it would look like? Is it even possible, in fact, to defeat the social metabolic system of capital with forms of struggle that are carried out only at the national level? Or, on the contrary, given the globalized shape of capitalism, has it not become even more urgent to create a new project of international working-class organization?

In order to explore these crucial questions, we must try to understand the new morphology of labour and some of its principal tendencies.

---

3 Ibid.
4 Karl Marx, "Provisional rules of the association", in *Karl Marx & Friedrich Engels, Collected Works*, vol. 20 (London: Lawrence & Wishart, 1976), 14–15.
5 Ibid., 15–16.

2 The New Morphology of Labour: Informality, Casualisation, Infoproletariat, and Value

Particularly since the widespread restructuring of capital, unleashed on a global scale in the early 1970s, the contemporary world of production has shown increased levels of casualisation of workers.[6] Work has become more and more destructive. As new mechanisms for extracting surplus labour are generated, jobs become more precarious, and masses of workers become disposable and unemployed. This has a downward effect on the wages of workers who are employed. The latest global crisis has amplified this effect. We now witness a huge 'waste' of human labour power, as the secure industrial jobs that were typical during much of the 20th century have become increasingly scarce.

Information and Communication Technologies (ICT) have invaded the world of commodities, providing greater *intellectual* capability (here understood in its narrow meaning given by the market). In this universe characterized by the subsumption of labour to the machine, stable work – associated with Taylorism/Fordism – is being replaced by *atypical work*, outsourced work, 'cooperativism', 'entrepreneurship', 'volunteer labour', etc. At the same time, this new morphology of labour has been expanding the range of *invisible labour*, using new and old mechanisms of labour-intensification. It is as if all possible activities – whether manual or intellectual – were converted into generators of surplus-value. The most important example is that of the service sector: whereas in the early period of industrial capitalism its activities were mostly unproductive, with the financialization of capital and with neoliberal privatization, the activities of the privatized service sector became productive for capital, even though they had the appearance of being unproductive. They also became generators of surplus-value.

Already in Marx's time certain service activities added value. This role is even more prevalent nowadays. Enterprises that provide services such as information and communications technology, telemarketing, fast food, hypermarkets, transport, etc., can no longer be considered as simply unproductive, but must be carefully analysed in relation to global production networks and the production of value.

In *Capital vol. 2*, Marx recognized that certain transport and warehousing activities could produce surplus value. In his words:

---

[6] See Ricardo Antunes, "La nueva morfologia del trabajo y sus principales tendencias", *Sociologia del Trabajo*, no. 74 (2012), 47–65.

> [...] what the transportation industry sells is change of location. The useful effect is inseparably connected with the process of transportation, i.e., the productive process of the transport industry. Men and goods travel together with the means of transportation, and this travelling, this locomotion, constitutes the process of production effected by these means. The useful effect can be consumed only during this process of production. It does not exist as a utility different from this process, a use thing which does not function as an article of commerce, does not circulate as a commodity, until after it has been produced. But the exchange value of this useful effect is determined, like that of any other commodity, by the value of the elements of production (labour power and means of production) consumed in it plus the surplus value created by the surplus labour of the labourers employed in transportation.[7]

Thus, the theory of value does not lose its relevance. Instead, we witness new and more complex methods of extracting surplus-value, including in activities considered non-material in Marx's terms.[8]

Our hypothesis is that various service activities are taking on an increasing role in constituting value, insofar as, in their interaction with dead labour, they participate in the process of valorisation of capital. In the early stages of capitalism, productive activities (generators of value) were mainly linked to industry and agriculture, mostly excluding services.[9] With the new forms of interaction between material and non-material labour, as well as the prevalence of collective labour in global production networks, the production of surplus-value grew significantly beyond what was possible in the traditional factory.

Today, the new contingent of workers in information and communication technologies (ICT) has been called cybertariat (by Ursula Huws[10]) or infoproletariat (by Ruy Braga and myself[11]). Huws's study remains central for understanding the interactions between material and non-material labour, as well as their connections with value's new modalities. As we know, telecommunications

---

7   Karl Marx, "Capital. Volume 2: The Process of Circulation of Capital", in *Karl Marx & Friedrich Engels, Collected Works*, vol. 36 (London: Lawrence & Wishart, 1997), 62.
8   Karl Marx, "Capital. Volume 1: The Process of Production of Capital", in *Karl Marx & Friedrich Engels, Collected Works*, vol. 35 (London: Lawrence & Wishart, 1996), 509–10.
9   Ricardo Antunes, *The Meanings of Work* (Chicago: Haymarket, 2013), chapter 7.
10 Ursula Huws, *The Making of a Cybertariat: virtual work in a real world* (New York: Monthly Review Press, 2003).
11 Ricardo Antunes & Ruy Braga, ed., *Infoproletários: Degradação Real do Trabalho Virtual* (São Paulo: Boitempo, 2009).

privatization led to an intensified process of outsourcing and introduced multiple forms of labour casualisation and intensification of the labour process.

Contrary to what was argued in theories of 'post-industrial society' and creative 'informational activity', work in the telemarketing industry has been marked by a contradictory process, since

1. It combines 21st century technologies (ICT) with 20th century working conditions.
2. It combines strategies of toyotised flexibility[12] with Taylorist rigidity.
3. It combines group work with the individualization of labour relations, encouraging both cooperation and competition between workers.

A preliminary phenomenology of labour informality demonstrates a sharp increase in the number of workers subjected to a succession of short-term contracts: they have neither stability nor formal status; they work in temporary activities, under the direct threat of unemployment. Workforce casualisation has been a central mechanism used by capital to intensify the rhythms and motions of labour, and thereby to extract more value from it.

Otherwise, why, in the middle of São Paulo, the most important industrial area of Brazil, would there exist today a 17-hour shift in the clothing industry, to be performed by Bolivian or Peruvian or other Latin American immigrant workers, who are informally hired and controlled by usually Korean or Chinese employers? We can also cite the case of African workers who pack textile and clothing products in Bom Retiro and Brás, small businesses in the city of São

---

12   Toyotism, the Japanese model for the expansion and consolidation of monopolistic industrial capitalism, is a form of labour organization that emerged in Toyota after 1945, and that rapidly expanded amongst other large Japanese companies. It differs from Fordism in the following ways: it is a form of production closely tied to demand that seeks to respond to the most individualized needs of the consumer-market; it is based on team-work, with cross-functional teams; the production process is flexible, allowing a worker to simultaneously operate various machines (at Toyota, on average five machines); it is based on the just-in-time principle, the best possible use of production time; it works according to the kanban system, command-tags or -boards for the replacement of parts and stock (under Toyotism, stocks are minimal when compared with Fordism); firms have a horizontal structure, as opposed to the vertical Fordist one; this horizontalization extends to subcontracted firms, leading to the expansion of these methods and procedures across the whole network of suppliers. Thus, flexibilization, subcontracting, total-quality control, kanban, just-in-time production, Kaizen, teamwork, the elimination of waste, 'participatory management' and enterprise unionism, among many other features, become part of the wider arena of the productive process; and quality-control circles (QCCs) are instituted – groups of workers who are encouraged by management to discuss their work and performance with a view to improving productivity. See Antunes, *The Meanings of Work*, chapter 4, 38–9.

Paulo, whose products for the African market are produced by arduous manual labour.

Other examples can be taken from the sugar agribusiness sector. Even though there is some formal labour in this sector, the rights of *bóias-frias* [rural laborers] continue to be circumvented. Rural laborers cut ten tons of sugarcane per day in the State of São Paulo and as much as 18 tons per day in the Northeastern region. Their workdays are exhausting, and their production is often undercounted by management. This scenario of work-intensification causes many fatalities among workers. Between 2003 and 2008, some 21 cane-cutters died from overwork in the State of São Paulo).[13]

In Japan, there is the recent case of *cyber-refugees* – young workers from the outskirts of Tokyo who do not have money to rent rooms. They stay in cyber-cafés at night to rest, use the Internet, and search for new contingent jobs. The best-known example is that of young workers in various parts of the world (known as *Dekasegis* in Japan) who migrate to cities in search of jobs. Without fixed residences, they sleep and rest in small rooms (glass capsules). I call them *encapsulated workers*.

In China, since the beginning of the century, there have been high rates of unemployment as transnational capital stretches to the limit the *super-exploitation* of the working class. The case of Foxconn is illuminating. Foxconn, a computing and information technology enterprise, is an example of Electronic Contract Manufacturing (ECM), a firm that assembles electronic products by subcontracting from Apple, Nokia and other transnationals. At its Longhua plant where the iPhone is assembled, there have been several suicides among the workforce since 2010, most caused by the intense exploitation and isolation of the work.

According to Pun Ngai and Jenny Chan

> the Foxconn tragedy has been dubbed the 'suicide express' by Chinese and international media. In the first eight months of 2010, a startling 17 young workers attempted or committed suicide at the Foxconn production facilities in China, bringing worldwide attention to all Foxconn's customers. 13 died, while four survived their injuries. All were between 17 and 25 years old [...] and their loss called upon concerned academics to closely study the changing pattern of global capital accumulation and its impacts on workers. Foxconn is a microcosm of the conditions that

---

13 See Ricardo Antunes, *Riqueza e Miséria do Trabalho no Brasil II* (São Paulo: Boitempo, 2013), chapter 17.

dominate the lives of Chinese migrant workers. When Time magazine nominated workers in China as runners-up to the 2009 Person of the Year, the editor commented that Chinese workers have brightened the future of humanity by "leading the world to economic recovery." The new generation of Chinese migrant workers, however, seem to perceive themselves as losing their futures. More than 900,000 young workers, who have been placed in the 'best' Foxconn factory-cum-dormitory environment, seemed only to show more anxieties, and see fewer alternatives, than their peers.[14]

This pattern is repeated in many other plants across China. According to SACOM (Students and Scholars against Corporate Misbehaviour), at the beginning of 2010, Foxconn workers work an average of 12 hours per day with a basic monthly wage of 900 yuan (just under US$150) which can reach 2,000 yuan for extra hours or for more strenuous work.

Immigrants are perhaps the most conspicuous victims of the structural trend toward casualisation. Given the enormous growth of the new informal proletariat, including the manufacturing and services subproletariat, new jobs are being filled by *Gastarbeiter* in Germany, *lavoratori in nero* in Italy, Mexican immigrants in the United States, East European immigrants (from Poland, Hungary, Romania, and Albania) in western Europe, *Dekasegis* in Japan, Bolivians and Africans in Brazil, and so on.

The cleavages that exist today between stable and precarious workers, men and women, young and elderly, white, black and Indian, and between skilled and unskilled workers are expressions of the new morphology of labour. Pietro Basso, who has studied this phenomenon in Europe, summarizes the reality as follows:

> once a continent of emigrants and settlers, as it had been for centuries, Western Europe has become a land of an increased flow of immigration from the entire globe. Today, 30 million immigrants live on its territory. And if we add to the immigrants without citizenship those who have obtained citizenship in one of the European countries, the total reaches 50 million, about 15 percent of the entire population of '15-Europe' [referring to when the EU consisted of 15 countries].[15]

---

14 See Pun Ngai & Jenny Chan, *The Advent of Capital Expansion in China: A Case Study of Foxconn Production and the Impacts on its Workers*, Accessed 10 October 2020, http://rdln.files.wordpress.com/2012/01/pun-ngai_chan-jenny_on-foxconn.pdf.

15 Pietro Basso, "L'immigrazione in Europa: caratteristiche e prospettive", Università Ca' Foscari Venezia (working paper), 1.

Among the immigrants, 22 percent come from Africa, 16 percent from Asia – half of these from the Far East (mainly China), and the other half from the Indian subcontinent. Fifteen percent are from Central and South America, and the remaining 45–47 percent come from other European countries, including those outside the EU (e.g., Turkey, the Balkans, Ukraine, Russia).[16]

Immigrant workers are paid the lowest wages and work during the least desired times, at night and on weekends. Yet Basso states that it is not about

> [...] 'just' overexploitation. In Europe, the whole existence of immigrants and their children is marked by *discrimination*. There is discrimination at the workplace, or when looking for a job, for unemployment insurance, and for retirement. Immigrants are discriminated against when they apply for housing benefits, when they must pay the highest rents to inhabit dilapidated dwellings in the most degraded areas. In fact, they suffer discrimination even in schools (in Germany there are very few children of immigrants who go to university; in Italy 42.5 percent of students who are children of immigrants are behind in their studies). They are discriminated against in their chances to reunite with their families, and, especially if they are Islamic, they suffer religious discrimination as well (being regarded as potential 'terrorists').[17]

Immigrants are thus at once the "*most unprotected* and the *most global*" category of worker. Hence, they constitute a sector of the working-class which is, "objectively and more than any other, the carrier of equalitarian and antiracist aspirations, even amid a plethora of contradictions, opportunism and individualism." They thus become "a collective subject which carries a need for social emancipation", as they refuse to "passively accept the condition of legal, material, social, cultural inferiority" associated with their immigrant status.[18] Citing the Italian case, Basso stresses that there have been some successful experiences of unionised immigrants. If, in the beginning, immigrants resorted to unions for aid, with the passage of time and with the consolidation of their presence in the workplace, they increasingly participate in union activities, as they come to represent the general interests of workers.[19]

---

16   Ibid.
17   Ibid.
18   Ibid., 6.
19   Ibid., 8. See also Pietro Basso & Fabio Perocco, *Razzismo di stato: Stati Uniti* (Milan: Angeli, 2010).

The recent demonstrations in Europe by immigrant workers and unemployed youth are emblematic. Precarious workers in Portugal organized a movement called *Precári@s Inflexíveis* [literally, Inflexible Precarious Workers].[20] Their *Manifesto* affirms the following:

> We are precarious in work and in life. We work without contract or on short-term contracts. [We have] temporary, uncertain jobs, without guarantees. We are call-centre workers, interns, unemployed people, independent workers, immigrant workers, casual workers, student-workers [...] We are not represented in statistics [...] We live off filler jobs. We can hardly provide a home. We can't take leave; we can't have children or become sick. Not to mention the right to strike. 'Flexicurity'? The 'flexi' is for us, while the 'security' is for our bosses. This 'modernization' is tricky and it has been planned and implemented by businessmen and Government, hand in hand. We are in the shadows but we are not silent. We won't stop fighting for fundamental rights alongside the workers in Portugal or abroad. This struggle is not about trade-union or government statistics [...] We don't fit in those figures. We won't let our conditions be forgotten. And using the same force with which we are attacked by our bosses, we will respond and reinvent our struggle. In the end, there are many more of us than of them. Yes, we are precarious, but we are inflexible.[21]

They are *discriminated against but not submissive;* as members of the working class, they seek to improve their living conditions *through work*. Immigrant workers in Western Europe are perhaps the tip of the iceberg, in terms of their working conditions and the precariousness of their jobs.

The new era of *structural casualisation of labour*, in sum, has these features:
1. Erosion of contracted and regulated work, and its replacement by various forms of atypical, precarious and 'volunteer' employment;
2. Creation of bogus cooperative societies, aimed at further squeezing wages by eroding workers' rights and intensifying exploitation;
3. Configuring 'entrepreneurship' as a hidden form of wage-labour, by proliferating various forms of wages, schedules, and functional or organizational flexibility;

---

20 [*Translator's note*: The @ symbol is used in Portuguese (and Spanish) to combine the masculine "o" with the feminine "a."].
21 "Manifesto Precário", Precári@s Inflexíveis, Accessed 10 October 2020, http://www.precarios.net/manifesto-precario/.

4. An ever more intense degradation of immigrant labour on a global scale. In the last few decades, we have been experiencing new forms of casualisation, a phase of 'toyotised' flexibility, which displays both continuity and discontinuity in relation to the Taylorist-Fordist modality. On the one hand, there are more highly skilled jobs for a reduced contingent (as exemplified by the workers of software industries and Information and Communication technology companies); on the other hand, work is increasingly unstable for a growing number of workers at the other end of the spectrum. Meanwhile, in the *middle* of the pyramid, we find hybridity, i.e., skilled labour that may disappear or be eroded by the temporal and spatial changes that have affected production and services worldwide.

Casualisation of labour seems to have become a constitutive feature of capital accumulation. The various manifestations of informality/casualisation entail a break with contractual obligations and regulations of the labour power such as prevailed under the Taylorist/Fordist regime of the 20th century. Informalization/casualisation is an important instrument used by capital to increase the rate of exploitation of labour and to make jobs globally more precarious. Although casualisation is not synonymous with precariousness, they are interrelated, insofar as informality and casualisation deprive workers of rights.

In this sense, lean production, team work, layoffs, productivity increases, and subcontracting constitute a model of the flexible enterprise governed by organizational lyophilization.[22] Whereas during the apogee Taylorism/Fordism – the era of the mass working class – the strength of an enterprise was proportional to the number of its employees, one can say that in the era of lean production and flexible accumulation, the enterprises that stand out are those that combine the smallest number of workers with high rates productivity.

Understanding this process gives us better insight into why the world of labour tends increasingly toward informality: The shift from Taylorism/Fordism to flexible accumulation means that jobs are no longer tightly regulated.

How is it possible to organize this new proletariat? How can this growing sector of the working class advance toward class consciousness, under

---

[22] Lyophilization, or 'freeze-drying', is a dehydration process that works by freezing perishable material. The lyophilization metaphor is used to evoke the elimination of living labour that occurs during the restructuring of production. See Juan J. Castillo, *Sociologia del Trabajo Colección,* in *'Monografías' 152* (Madrid: Centro de Investigaciones Sociológicas, 1996), and "A la Búsqueda del Trabajo Perdido", in *Complejidad y Teoria Social,* ed. Alfonso Pérez-Agote and Ignacio Yucera (Madrid: CIS, 1996).

conditions of the transnationalization of capital? How can it link up with the more traditional sectors of the working class?

3 Conclusion

Just as capital is a global system, the world of labour and its challenges are also increasingly transnationalized. As yet, there has not arisen an international response on the part of the working-class. It keeps itself predominantly within its national structures, which pose enormous limitations on workers' action. As the space and time of production are reconfigured globally, there has been a process of both re-territorialization and de-territorialization. New industrial regions emerge and many disappear, at the same time that more and more factories become globalized.[23]

The centre of present-day social confrontation is given by the contradiction between *total social capital* and the *totality of labour*.[24] Therefore, just as capital makes use of its globalized mechanisms and international organs, so also must workers' struggle become – in the spirit of the IWA – increasingly international. On this terrain, as we know, capital is well ahead of labour in its level of solidarity and class-action. Yet it often happens that the success or failure of a strike in one or more countries depends upon the solidarity and action of workers in productive units of the same company elsewhere.

Existing international labour organizations nearly always have a traditional bureaucratic and institutionalized structure that leaves them incapable of offering an alternative social vision opposed to the logic of capital. They tend to assume a defensive stance or one that is subordinate to the logic of internationalization of capital, opposing merely some of its most dire consequences. The conflict between native (territorialized) and immigrant (de-territorialized) workers reflects the process of economic transnationalisation, to which the labour movement has been unable to provide a satisfactory response.

In this way, besides the cleavages that exist between secure and precarious workers, men and women, young and old people, native and immigrant, black and white, skilled and unskilled, 'included' and 'excluded', and many other examples to be found with the national space, the stratification and fragmentation of labour are also accentuated by the growing internationalization of capital. This broader, more complex and fragmented world of labour is

---

23 See Antunes, *The Meanings of Work*, 93–95.
24 See István Mészáros, *Beyond Capital: Towards a Theory of Transition* (London: Merlin Press, 1995).

manifested: 1) within particular groups or sectors of work; 2) between different groups of workers within the same national community; 3) between different national bodies of labour, pitted against one another by international capitalist competition; 4) between the labour power of advanced capitalist countries – relative beneficiaries of the global capitalist division of labour – and the relatively more exploited labour power of the 'Third World'; and 5) between employed workers and the unemployed, including those that are increasingly victims of the 'second industrial revolution'.[25]

The precarious workers struggle, as did workers during the Industrial Revolution, for basic workers' rights. The Fordist workers try to resist the complete destruction of their rights. These two basic poles of the same working-class face a future in which their prospects are bound together. The former – the 'disorganized' – seek a complete end to precarization and dream of a better world. The latter – the 'organized' – want to avoid being degraded to the status of the world's newly precarious.

Given that the destructive logic of capital is seemingly multiple but in essence unitary, if these vital poles of labour don't ally themselves organically, they will suffer the tragedy of greater precarization and complete dehumanization. If, on the other hand, they forge ties of solidarity, of common class-affiliation, and of a *new mode of being*, defining and planning their actions, they may have greater power than any other social force to demolish the social metabolism of capital and thereby begin delineating a *new way of life*.

We should recall, in closing, this decisive observation of the IWA, made even stronger now by the globalization of capital and of labour:

> one element of success they possess – numbers; but numbers weigh in the balance only if united by combination and led by knowledge. Past experience has shown how disregard of that bond of brotherhood which ought to exist between the workmen of different countries, and incite them to stand firmly by each other in all their struggles for emancipation, will be chastised by the common discomfiture of their incoherent efforts. This thought prompted the workingmen of different countries assembled on September 28, 1864, in public meeting at St. Martin's Hall, to found the International Association.[26]

The experience of the IWA, which for a long time appeared to have been buried, is being resurrected 150 years later.

---

25   Ibid., 929.
26   Marx, *"Inaugural Address"*.

Master References

Annunziato, Frank. "Il Fordismo nella Critica di Gramsci e nella Realtà Statunitense Contemporanea". *Critica Marxista,* no. 6 (1989).

Antunes, Ricardo & Braga, Ruy, ed. *Infoproletários: Degradação Real do Trabalho Virtual.* São Paulo: Boitempo, 2009.

Antunes, Ricardo. "La nueva morfologia del trabajo y sus principales tendencias". *Sociologia del Trabajo,* no. 74 (2012).

Antunes, Ricardo. "The New Morphology of Labour and its Main Trends: Informalisation, Precarisation, (Im)materiality and Value". *Critique,* vol. 44, no. 1–2 (2016).

Antunes, Ricardo. "The New Morphology of the Working Class in Contemporary Brazil". In *Socialist Register 2015: Transforming Classes,* edited by Leo Panitch and Greg Albo. London: Merlin Press, 2014.

Antunes, Ricardo. "The New Service Proletariat". *Monthly Review,* vol. 69 (2018).

Antunes, Ricardo. *O Caracol e sua Concha: Ensaios sobre a Nova Morfologia do Trabalho.* São Paulo: Boitempo, 2005.

Antunes, Ricardo. *O Novo Sindicalismo.* São Paulo: Scritta, 1991.

Antunes, Ricardo. *Riqueza e Miséria do Trabalho no Brasil.* São Paulo: Boitempo, 2006.

Antunes, Ricardo. *Riqueza e Miséria do Trabalho no Brasil II.* São Paulo: Boitempo, 2013.

Antunes, Ricardo. *The Meanings of Work.* Chicago: Haymarket, 2013.

Basso, Pietro & Perocco, Fabio. *Razzismo di stato: Stati Uniti.* Milan: Angeli, 2010.

Basso, Pietro. "L'immigrazione in Europa: caratteristiche e prospettive". Università Ca' Foscari Venezia (working paper).

Berggren, Christian. "New Production Concepts in Final Assembly: The Swedish Experience". In *The Transformation of Work: skill, flexibility, and the labour process,* edited by Stephen Wood. London: Unwin Hyman, 1989.

Berman, Marshall. *All that is Solid Melts into Air.* London: Penguin Books, 1988.

Bernardo, João. *Capital, Sindicatos, Gestores.* São Paulo: Vértice, 1987.

Bialakowsky, Alberto et al. "Dilución y Mutación del Trabajo en la Dominación Social Local". *Revista Herramienta,* no. 23 (2003).

Bihr, Alain. "Le Prolétariat Dans Tous Ses Éclats". *Le Monde Diplomatique,* n. 444 (1991).

Bihr, Alain. *Du 'Grand Soir' a 'l' Alternative': le Mouvement Ouvrier Européen en Crise.* Paris: Les Éditions Ouvrières, 1991.

Bordieu, Pierre. *Distinction: A social critique of the judgement of taste.* Cambridge: Harvard University Press, 2002.

Bordogna, Lorenzo. " 'Arcipelago Cobas': Frammentazione della rappresentanza e conflitti di Lavoro". In *Política in Italia.* Bologna: Mulino Publisher, 1988.

Braverman, Harry. *Labor and Monopoly Capital.* New York: Monthly Review Press, 1974.

Castillo, Juan. "Sociologia del Trabajo". In *Colección 'Monografías' 152*. Madrid: Centro de Investigaciones Sociológicas, 1996.

Chesnais, François. *A Mundialização do Capital*. São Paulo: Editora Xamã, 1996.

Clarke, Simon. "The Crisis of Fordism or the Crisis of Social-Democracy?". *Telos*, no. 83 (1990).

Clash City Workers. *Dove Sono i Nostri: Lavoro, Classe e Movimenti nell'Itália della crisi*. Lucca: La Casa Usher, 2014.

Coriat, Benjamin. *El Taller y el Robot: Ensayos Sobre el Fordismo y la Producción en Masa en la Era de la Electrónica*. Ciudad de México: Siglo XXI, 1992.

Coriat, Benjamin. *Pensar al Revés: Trabajo y Organización em la Empresa Japonesa*. Ciudad de México: Siglo XXI, 1992.

Davis, Mike. *Planet of Slums*. London: Verso, 2017.

Freeman, Richard. "Pueden Sobrevivir los Sindicatos en la Sociedad Pos-industrial". *Simpósio Internacional sobre las Perspectivas Futuras del Sindicalismo*. Confédération des Syndicats Chrétiens, Brussels (1986).

Freyssenet, Michel. "A Divisão Capitalista do Trabalho". *Tempo Social*, vol. 1, no. 2 (1989).

Freyssinet, Jacques. "Syndicalismes en Europe". *Le Mouvement Social*, no. 162 (1993).

Gorz, André. "O Futuro da Classe Operária". *Revista Internacional, Quinzena*, no. 101 (1990).

Gorz, André. "Pourquoi la Societé Salariale a Besoin de Nouveux Valets". *Le Monde Diplomatique*, no. 22 (1990).

Gorz, André. "The New Agenda". *New Left Review*, no. 184 (1990).

Gorz, André. *Farewell to the Working Class: an Essay on Post-Industrial Socialism*. London: Pluto Press, 1982.

Gorz, André. *The immaterial*. London: Seagull Books, 2010.

Gounet, Thomas. "Luttes Concurrentielles et Stratégies d'Accumulation dans l'Industries Automobile". *Études Marxistes*, no. 10 (1991).

Gounet, Thomas. "Penser à l'Envers ... Le Capitalisme". *Études Marxistes*, no. 14 (1992).

Gramsci, Antonio. "Americanism and Fordism". In *The Gramsci Reader*, edited by David Forgarcs. New York: NYU Press, 2000.

Habermas, Jürgen. "Technology and Science as 'Ideology' ". In *Toward a Rational Society: Student Protest, Science, and Politics*. Boston: Beacon Press, 1989.

Habermas, Jürgen. "The New Obscurity". In *The New Conservatism: Cultural Criticism and the Historians' Debate*. Cambridge: Polity Press, 1989.

Habermas, Jürgen. *The Theory of Communicative Action vol. 1: Reason and the Rationalization of Society*. London: Polity Press, 1991.

Habermas, Jürgen. *The Theory of Communicative Action vol. 2: The Critique of Functionalist Reason*. London: Polity Press, 1992.

Harvey, David. *The Condition of Postmodernity: An Enquiry into the Origins of Cultural Change*. Oxford: Blackwell Publishers, 1990.

Heller, Agnes. "El futuro de las relaciones entre los sexos". In *La Revolución de la Vida Cotidiana*. Barcelona: Ed. Península, 1982.

Heller, Agnes. "Paradigma dela Produzione e Paradigma del Lavoro". *Critica Marxista*, no. 4 (1981).

Heller, Agnes. *Everyday Life*. London: Routledge & Kegan Paul, 1984.

Heller, Agnes. *The Theory of Need in Marx*. London: Allison & Busby, 1974.

Hirata, Helena. "Trabalho, Família e Relações Homem/Mulher: Reflexões a Partir do Caso Japonês". *Revista Brasileira de Ciências Sociais*, vol. 1, no. 2 (1986).

Huws, Ursula. *The Making of a Cybertariat: virtual work in a real world*. New York: Monthly Review Press, 2003.

Ianni, Octávio. *A Sociedade Global*. Rio de Janeiro: Civilização Brasileira, 1992.

Kelly, John. *Labour and the Unions*. London: Verso, 1987.

Kurz, Robert. *Der Kollaps der Modernisierung: vom Zusammenbruch des Kasernen Sozialismus zur Krise der Weltokonomie*. Frankfurt am Main: Vito von Eichborn GmbH & Co. Verlag, 1991.

Kurz, Robert. *O Colapso da Modernização: Da Derrocada do Socialismo de Caserna à Crise da Economia Mundial*. São Paulo: Paz e Terra, 1992.

Kurz, Robert. *Os Últimos Combates*. Rio de Janeiro: Vozes, 1997.

Lojkine, Jean. *A Classe Operária em Mutações*. São Paulo: Oficina de Livros, 1990.

Lojkine, Jean. *A Revolução Informacional*. São Paulo: Editora Cortez, 1995.

Lukács, György. "The 'Vienna Paper': The Ontological Foundations of Human Thinking and Action". In *Lukács's Last Autocriticism: the Ontology*, edited by Ernst Joós. Atlantic Highlands: Humanities Press, 1982.

Lukács, György. *Ontologia dell'Essere Sociale I*. Roma: Riuniti, 1976.

Lukács, György. *Ontologia dell'Essere Sociale II, vol. 1*. Roma: Riuniti, 1981.

Lukács, György. *Ontologia dell'Essere Sociale II, vol. 2*. Roma: Riuniti, 1981.

Lukács, György. *The Ontology of Social Being: 3. Labour*. London: Merlin Press, 1980.

Mallet, Serge. *The New Working Class*. Nottingham: Spokesman Books, 1973.

Mandel, Ernest. "Marx, La Crise Actuelle et L'Avenir du Travail Humain". *Quatrième Internationale*, no. 2 (1986).

Mandel, Ernst. "Marx, the Present Crisis and the Future of Labour". In *Socialist Register 1985–1986*, edited by Ralph Miliband et al. London: Merlin Press, 1986.

Marx, Karl. "Capital. Volume 1: The Process of Production of Capital". In *Karl Marx & Friedrich Engels, Collected Works, vol. 35*. London: Lawrence & Wishart, 1996.

Marx, Karl. "Capital. Volume 2: The Process of Circulation of Capital". In *Karl Marx & Friedrich Engels, Collected Works, vol. 36*. London: Lawrence & Wishart, 1997.

Marx, Karl. "Capital. Volume 3: *The Process of Capitalist Production as a Whole*". In *Karl Marx & Friedrich Engels, Collected Works, vol. 37*. London: Lawrence & Wishart, 1998.

Marx, Karl. "Chapter Six. Results of the Direct Production Process". In *Karl Marx & Friedrich Engels, Collected Works, vol. 34*. London: Lawrence & Wishart, 1994.

Marx, Karl. "Inaugural Address of the International Working Men's Association, The First International". In *Karl Marx & Friedrich Engels, Collected Works*, vol. 20 London: Lawrence & Wishart, 1976.

Marx, Karl. "Outlines of the Critique of Political Economy". In *Karl Marx & Friedrich Engels, Collected Works*, vol. 29. London: Lawrence & Wishart, 1987.

Marx, Karl. "Provisional rules of the association". In *Karl Marx & Friedrich Engels, Collected Works*, vol. 20. London: Lawrence & Wishart, 1976.

Marx, Karl. "Theses on Feuerbach". In *Karl Marx & Friedrich Engels, Collected Works*, vol. 5. London: Lawrence & Wishart, 1976.

Mészáros, István. "Il Rinnovamento del Marxismo e l'Attualità Storica dell'Ofensiva Socialista". *Problemi del Socialismo*, no. 23 (1982).

Mészáros, István. "Marxism Today: an Interview with István Mészáros". Interview by Chris Arthur and Joseph McCarney. *Monthly Review*, vol. 39/3 (1993).

Mészáros, István. "The Division of Labour and the Post-Capitalist State". *Monthly Review*, vol. 37/3 (1987).

Mészáros, István. *A Necessidade do Controle Social*. São Paulo: Ensaio, 1989.

Mészáros, István. *Beyond Capital: Towards a Theory of Transition*. London: Merlin Press, 1995.

Mészáros, István. *The Necessity of Social Control*. New York: Monthly Review Press, 2015.

Mészáros, István. *The Power of Ideology*. London: Harvester Wheatsheaf, 1989.

Murray, Fergus. "The Decentralization of Production – The Decline of the Mass-Collective Worker". *Capital & Class*, no. 19 (1983).

Ngai, Pun & Chan, Jenny. *The Advent of Capital Expansion in China: A Case Study of Foxconn Production and the Impacts on its Workers*, Accessed 10 October 2020, http://rdln.files.wordpress.com/2012/01/pun-ngai_chan-jenny_on-foxconn.pdf.

Offe, Claus & Berger, Johannes. "A Dinâmica do Desenvolvimento do Setor de Serviços". *Trabalho & Sociedade*, vol. 2 (1991).

Offe, Claus. "Trabalho como Categoria Sociológica Fundamental?". *Trabalho & Sociedade*, vol. 1 (1989).

Oliveira, Francisco de. "A Economia Política da Social-Democracia". *Revista USP*, no. 136 (1992).

Oliveira, Francisco de. "O Surgimento do Anti-Valor". *Novos Estudos Cebrap*, no. 22 (1988).

Pollert, Anna. "'Team work' on the Assembly Line: Contradiction and the Dynamics of Union Resilience". In *The New Workplace and Trade Unionism: Critical Perspectives on Work and Organization*, edited by Peter Ackers, Paul Smith & Chris Smith. London: Routledge, 1996.

Rodrigues, Leôncio M. "A Crise do Sindicalismo no Primeiro Mundo". *Folha de São Paulo*, 22 March, 1993.

Rodrigues, Leôncio M. "A Sindicalização da Classe Média". *Folha de São Paulo*, 24 May, 1993.

Sabel, Charles & Piore, Michael. *The Second Industrial Divide: Possibilities for Prosperity*. New York: Basic Books, 1984.

Santos, Vinícius. *Trabalho Imaterial e Teoria do Valor em Marx*. São Paulo: Expressão Popular, 2013.

Schaff, Adam. *A Sociedade Informática*. São Paulo: Brasiliense/Unesp, 1990.

Standing, Guy. *The Precariat: The New Dangerous Class*. London: Bloomsbury, 2011.

Stuppini, Andrea. "Chi Sono e che Cosa Vogliono i Nuovi Operai". *Mondo Operaio*, no. 2, Anno 44 (1991).

Taylor, Frederick Winslow. *Principles of Scientific Management*. New York and London: Harper & Brothers, 1911.

Tertulian, Nicolas. "Le Concept d'Aliénation chez Heidegger et Lukács". *Archives de Philosophie: Reserches et Documentation*, no. 56 (1993).

Tosel, André. "Centralité et Non-Centralité du Travail ou La Passion des Hommes Superflus". In *La Crise du Travail. Actuel Marx Confrontation*, edited by Jacques Bidet & Jacques Texier. Paris: Presses Universitaries de France, 1995.

Touraine, Alain. "Os Novos Conflitos Sociais". *Lua Nova*, no. 17 (1989).

Vasapollo, Luciano. *O Trabalho Atípico e a Precariedade*. São Paulo: Expressão Popular, 2005.

Vincent, Jean-Marie. "Les Automatismes Sociaux et le 'General Intellect' ". *Paradigmes du Travail, Futur Antérieur*, no. 16 (1993).

Visser, Jelle. "Syndicalisme et Désyndicalisation". *Le Mouvement Social*, no. 162 (1993).

Watanabe, Ben. "Karoshi, Made in Japan". *Revista Internacional, Quinzena*, no. 167 (1993).

Watanabe, Ben. "Toyotismo: Um Novo Padrão Mundial de Produção?". *Revista dos Metalúrgicos*, (December 1993).

Index

agribusiness sector   101, 121
alienation   7, 21, 59n28, 62–64, 83, 91
Annunziato, Frank   1, 5n1, 8, 8n7, 14n25, 25, 25n2, 29n18
atypical work   85, 95, 118
automation   x, 5, 10, 26, 34n32, 56–57

Basso, Pietro   122n15, 122–123, 123n19
Bihr, Alain   1, 24n1, 26, 26n7, 26n8, 26n9, 28n15, 34n31, 40n6, 40–41, 41n13, 81n44
Braga, Ruy   74, 74n24, 90n8, 102n8, 119, 119n11
Braverman, Harry   78, 78n34
Brazil   xii, xiii–1, 37n1, 41–42, 46, 64, 75, 78n38, 81, 85, 88–90, 93–94, 99–101, 105n2, 120, 122

Chesnais, François   78n37
class-that-lives-from-labour   x, xiii–1, 5, 23, 28, 35–36, 40, 43, 45, 52, 58, 60–61, 64, 80, 96, 98, 112
commodity fetishism   21, 105
cooperatives   85, 89
cooperativism   85, 118
Coriat, Benjamin   1, 6n1, 6–7, 7n3, 12n17, 12–13, 13n22, 13n24, 14n25, 14n26, 14–15, 15n28, 17n37, 18n41, 17–20, 34n32
crisis of labouring society   1, 57n26, 112

Davis, Mike   94, 94n15
Dekasegis   94, 100, 121–122
deskilling   29, 34n32, 34–35, 35n35, 47
domestic outworkers   8

Engels, Friedrich   23n49, 30n22, 32n25, 47n2, 53n16, 70n6, 70n7, 70n9, 73n20, 81, 96, 97n2, 103n10, 111n20, 116n2, 117n4, 119n7, 119n8
England   40, 69, 79, 81, 109
entrepreneurship   85, 118, 124

financialization   xiii, 92, 118
flexibilization   5, 11n16, 15–16, 68, 85–86, 90, 95, 120n12
flexible accumulation   9–11, 88–89, 100, 125
flexible specialization   5, 7–8

Fordism   5n1, 7n4, 5–10, 12, 14–15, 20–21, 21n44, 34, 40, 46, 62, 83–84, 89, 100, 118, 120n12, 125
Foxconn   77n33, 121–122, 122n14, 132
free time   52–54, 58, 63

gender   28, 64, 67n3, 80, 82, 93
Gorz, André   1, 11n16, 23n46, 26n6, 26–27, 27n12, 33n26, 49, 49n7, 51n11, 51–52, 54n18, 54n18, 57n26, 58n27, 61, 62n31, 62n31, 67n2, 76n30, 92n12, 101, 101n6, 111
Gounet, Thomas   1, 5n1, 13n20, 13n23, 14n25, 14n26, 15n29, 14–16, 16n31, 16n32
Gramsci, Antonio   5n1, 8n7, 14n25, 21, 21n44, 25n2, 29n18, 113

Habermas, Jürgen   23n47, 49n7, 49–51, 51n10, 51n12, 57n26, 67n2, 74n21, 97, 97n3, 101, 101n6, 111
Harvey, David   1, 5n1, 9n10, 10n13, 9–11, 27, 27n11, 28n16, 34, 35n33, 35n34
Heller, Agnes   28n17, 51, 51n13, 55n19, 64n35
Hirata, Helena   27, 27n13, 28n17
Huws, Ursula   74, 74n23, 83n1, 90, 90n7, 102n7, 119, 119n10

immaterial production   73–76
immigrant   24, 40, 42, 45, 69, 79–81, 93–95, 99–101, 104, 120, 122–126
indigenous peoples   95
individualization of work relations   42
industrial workers   1, 21, 23–26, 29, 33–34, 36, 44, 73
industrialization   x–1, 42, 106, 108
infoproletariat   74, 90, 102, 119
international division of labour   64, 81, 88, 93
International Workingmen's Association   116–117, 126–127
Italy   xii, xiii, 8, 24–25, 28–29, 39, 41, 44, 51n11, 68–69, 69n5, 79, 84, 94, 100, 122–123

Japanese model   12, 14, 16, 0020518–20, 34, 43, 120n12
just in time   14–15, 88

INDEX

kanban 12, 14–15, 88, 120n12
karoshi 18
Kurz, Robert 1, 19n43, 23n48, 29n21, 49, 49n6, 49n8, 52n14, 57n26, 58n26, 67n2, 78n37, 97, 97n4, 101, 101n6, 105n2, 105–106, 106n3, 111n21, 108–114

labour
  abstract x, 0044947–54, 57n26, 57–58, 60, 91, 97, 99, 106–107, 111–112
  casualisation xii, 88–89, 91, 120, 124–125
  concrete x, 48, 50–52, 54, 56, 58, 60
  deregulation 26, 42, 88–89
  heteronomous 51–52
  immaterial 67, 76, 86–87, 91–92, 97, 102
  intermittent 69, 82
  process 6, 8, 11n16, 21, 32, 35n35, 37n1, 47, 55n19, 63–64, 75, 98, 103, 120
  transversalities 93, 95, 103
  women 11n16, 24, 27–28, 36, 40, 60, 79, 86–88, 93–95, 122, 126
labour movement 53, 109–110, 112, 126
law of value xii, 47, 67, 76–77, 92–93, 101–103
lifetime job 13, 18
Lojkine, Jean 1, 33n29, 68n4, 90, 90n9, 103, 103n9
Lukács, György 23, 23n49, 55, 55n19, 55n20, 56n23, 63, 63n32, 92, 92n11, 97n2, 111, 113

Mandel, Ernest 1, 33n28, 57, 57n24, 97n2
Marx, Karl ix, x, 10, 21, 23, 23n49, 30n22, 31n23, 30–32, 32n25, 33n28, 47n2, 49, 51, 53, 53n16, 55n19, 57, 57n24, 62n31, 64n35, 70n6, 70n7, 70n8, 70n9, 71n10, 73n17, 73n20, 74n25, 74n26, 70–76, 76n29, 76n32, 80–81, 81n43, 84, 97n2, 97n2, 96–99, 103, 103n10, 103n11, 105, 109, 111n20, 111–113, 116, 116n2, 117n4, 117–119, 119n7, 119n8, 127n26
Mercantilism 106, 113
Mészáros, István 1, 22, 22n45, 36n36, 44n19, 48n5, 53n17, 59, 59n28, 60n29, 74n22, 78n37, 101, 101n5, 126n24
middle class 41, 77–78

OECD 45, 109
Offe, Claus 1, 23n47, 29n20, 49n7, 49–50, 57n26, 111
omnilaterality 49, 56, 60, 62, 112

outsourcing 10, 15, 24, 26, 34, 41–42, 45, 58, 60, 77n33, 77–78, 85, 87–90, 95, 100, 102, 118, 120

part-time job 24, 26–28, 35, 40–41, 45, 67, 69, 87, 93, 95, 99
Piore, Michael 5n1, 7n2, 5–8, 10, 10n12
polyvalence 14, 34
precariat 69, 77–82
precarious work 24, 26
precarious workers 62, 69, 80, 95, 104, 122, 124, 126–127
production processes 5, 8, 10, 89
productive restructuring 83, 88, 90, 92
putting out system 8, 89

Quality Control Circles 6, 15, 17

relative surplus population 81
resistance xiii, 14n25, 22, 58, 111
robots 32–33
rural laborers 121
Russian Revolution 113

Sabel, Charles 5n1, 7n2, 5–8, 10, 10n12
Schaff, Adam 1, 26n4
service sector 24–25, 28–29, 36, 58, 67, 72–73, 76–78, 91, 118
sexual division of labour 67n3, 93
social division of labour 54, 60n29
social movements 22, 39n5, 44, 46, 79
social protection system 90
Standing, Guy 78n36, 78–79, 79n40, 79n41
strike 13, 34, 41–42, 61, 78, 81, 104, 124, 126
structural unemployment 11, 20, 24, 26, 42, 46, 60, 62–63, 88, 94, 114
struggle 9, 22, 28, 42, 52–53, 58, 60, 80, 82, 99, 104, 109, 112, 114, 116–117, 124, 126–127
  anti-racist 58
  feminist 58
  LGBT 58
  youth 58
sub-contracting 10, 16, 35
sub-proletarianization ix, 24, 26–28, 35
subproletariat 24, 34, 41, 61, 87, 94, 99, 122

Taylorism 5–6, 83–84, 89, 100, 118, 125
technology
  development 6, 8–9, 32, 35, 46, 60, 63, 107
  revolution 26, 56

temporary workers   16, 27, 90
Tertulian, Nicolas   91, 92n11
theory of value   xii, 67, 70, 74, 76, 76n31, 87, 101, 103, 112, 119
Third Italy   5–6, 11, 84
Tosel, André   76n32, 103n11
Touraine, Alain   1, 51n11, 51n11
Toyota   12–14, 16–17, 20–21, 42, 47, 76n31, 84, 87, 93, 97, 103, 120n12
Toyotism   5–6, 14n25, 12–21, 34, 45, 61–62, 88, 100, 120n12
trade union   xiii, 5, 8, 13, 17, 37, 39n5, 39–46, 69, 80
  crisis   37, 44, 46
  enterprise trade unionism   13, 20, 43, 120n12
  unionisation rate   38, 40
transport sector   72
Trotsky, Leon   113

Uber   68
uberization   69
unemployment   20, 27, 34, 42, 58–59, 61, 69n5, 79, 84–86, 89, 94–95, 99, 103–104, 118, 120–121, 123–124, 127

Vasapollo, Luciano   85n4, 95, 95n17, 102n8

welfare state   19, 24, 43, 50n9, 50–51, 80, 82, 84
Western Marxism   113
working class   ix, x, xiii–2, 9, 14n25, 19, 19n43, 21, 23n46, 23–24, 27, 29, 33–34, 36, 40–42, 45, 49, 49n7, 52, 52n14, 54n18, 61n30, 59–62, 62n31, 64, 73, 78n38, 78–82, 85–86, 90, 96–100, 109, 114, 116–117, 121, 124–125, 130
  end of the working class   1
working from home   58

Printed in the United States
by Baker & Taylor Publisher Services